BRICS Odyssey: Navigating a Multipolar World

From Vision to Reality: How BRICS Is Shaping Tomorrow

Bahaa G Arnouk

ISBN: 978-1-0683791-0-9

Book Cover by Bahaa Arnouk

1st edition 2025

Table of Contents

Introduction

The world is shifting. Old certainties are fading, and a new era is unfolding—one where influence is no longer concentrated in a single power center but shared among nations rising to shape their own destinies. In this evolving global landscape, **BRICS Odyssey: Navigating a Multipolar World** tells the story of an alliance that is more than just an economic bloc—it is a force of transformation, a coalition of nations determined to unlock new possibilities, redefine partnerships, and contribute to a future that is more dynamic, balanced, and inclusive.

BRICS is a movement of reinvention. It began as a bold concept in the early 2000s, a vision that many saw as ambitious, perhaps even improbable. Few could have predicted that Brazil, Russia, India, China, and later South Africa—nations spread across continents, with diverse histories, cultures, and economies—would come together to form an alliance that has grown to influence global trade, finance, and governance. And yet, they have. Today, BRICS stands at the heart of a multipolar world, proving that alternative pathways to growth, collaboration, and economic resilience are not only possible but essential.

This is not a story of opposition—it is a story of expansion. **BRICS Odyssey** is about the collective ambition of emerging markets to harness their strengths, build new bridges of cooperation, and navigate a world where influence is increasingly distributed. The BRICS nations are not merely adapting to change; they are actively shaping it. Their partnership is founded on a core belief: that sovereignty and cooperation are not mutually exclusive, that diversity is an asset, and that the future of global governance should reflect the realities of a rapidly changing world.

Each BRICS nation brings something unique to this shared odyssey. Brazil's vast natural wealth and pioneering sustainability efforts position it as a leader in green innovation. Russia's strategic adaptability and energy influence make it a crucial player in global markets. India's technological revolution and thriving digital economy showcase the power of innovation-driven growth. China, a manufacturing and financial giant, exemplifies the strength of long-term vision and economic scale. South Africa, as a vital gateway to the African continent, serves as a bridge between regions, fostering deeper global partnerships. Together, these nations form a dynamic mosaic of ambition, resilience, and forward momentum.

But the story of BRICS does not stop here. It is evolving. With the expansion of **BRICS+**, new voices have entered the dialogue, expanding the coalition's scope and reach. Nations like Iran, Egypt, Ethiopia, and the UAE have joined the conversation, strengthening the bloc's economic and geopolitical influence. Today, BRICS+ represents nearly half of the world's population and a significant share of global GDP. Its presence is more than symbolic—it signals a world where economic and political engagement is becoming more diverse, where no single path dictates success, and where emerging economies are forging their own futures.

BRICS Odyssey is an invitation to explore this unfolding transformation. This book delves into the economic landscapes of BRICS and its extended partners, uncovering the challenges they face, the opportunities they seize, and the innovations they drive. From game-changing financial systems to ambitious infrastructure projects, from energy revolutions to digital breakthroughs, BRICS is crafting a new narrative—one of progress, partnership, and possibility.

This is a book of exploration—a journey through the rise of BRICS and the ever-expanding possibilities of a multipolar world. It is a chronicle of ambition, adaptation, and cooperation among nations that refuse to be confined by past paradigms. It is a testament to the idea that economic and political influence is not static but fluid, shaped by those who dare to reimagine what is possible.

So step into this journey with me. Let us explore the **BRICS Odyssey**—a story of nations rewriting the rules, embracing transformation, and forging a future where global progress is not the privilege of a few but the right of many.

This is the story of BRICS—its evolution, its ambitions, and its role in shaping the world of tomorrow

Chapter (1)

BRICS and BRICS+: Redefining Global Power and Unity in a Multipolar World

"The BRICS Still Don't Matter."

Jim O'Neill, Economist and Creator of the BRIC Acronym

BRICS, an acronym coined by economist Jim O'Neill in 2001, initially served as a concept to highlight the burgeoning economic potential of four nations—Brazil, Russia, India, and China—that were on track to redefine the global economic order. At the time, these nations were characterized by rapid GDP growth, vast populations, and significant geographical and economic diversity. Whether or not the vision was not merely about recognizing growth but about acknowledging the shifting center of global economic gravity away from the traditional dominance of Western economies, in 2024 though, O'Neill believes that "*The BRICS Still Don't Matter*", and that "*The annual BRICS summit is an ideal occasion for political leaders like Vladimir Putin to promote a vision of a world that the United States does not lead*".

The journey from concept to coalition began with informal interactions, as foreign ministers of Brazil, Russia, India, and China met on the sidelines of the UN General Assembly in New York in 2006. These discussions laid the groundwork for a more formal dialogue on issues of shared interest, particularly the need to reform global financial and governance institutions like the International Monetary Fund (IMF) and the World Bank. By 2009, this grouping had transformed into an official coalition, with the first BRIC leaders' summit held on June 16, 2009, in Yekaterinburg, Russia.

The Yekaterinburg summit was a defining moment, as it was not only the official birth of BRIC but also a declaration of its intentions and principles. The summit's primary focus was addressing the aftermath of the 2008 global financial crisis, which exposed vulnerabilities in the Western-dominated financial system. BRIC leaders—Brazil's Luiz Inácio Lula da Silva, Russia's Dmitry Medvedev, India's Manmohan Singh, and China's Hu Jintao—called for a new global financial architecture that was more inclusive and representative of emerging economies. They emphasized the need for a "diverse, stable, and predictable" global reserve currency system, subtly critiquing the US dollar's dominance without directly opposing it.

During the summit, the founding principles of BRIC were articulated, emphasizing sovereignty, mutual respect, non-interference, equality, and mutual benefit. These principles formed the bedrock of the bloc's cooperative framework, underscoring a shared commitment to multilateralism and sustainable development. The leaders also highlighted the importance of creating mechanisms to enhance trade, investment, and financial collaboration among member states.

The inclusion of South Africa in 2010 was a pivotal moment in the bloc's evolution, expanding its reach to include a major African economy and transforming the grouping into BRICS. South Africa's entry marked a significant step toward inclusivity, aligning with the bloc's vision of representing the interests of diverse emerging markets and developing nations. It symbolized a commitment to addressing global economic disparities and ensuring a more balanced representation in international decision-making.

In subsequent years, BRICS established pioneering institutions that reflected its objectives of economic reform and global governance. The New Development Bank (NDB), launched in 2014, serves as a counterweight to Western-led financial institutions, funding sustainable infrastructure projects across the Global South. Similarly, the BRICS Contingent Reserve Arrangement (CRA) was created to provide liquidity support to members during financial crises, further underscoring the bloc's commitment to financial stability and resilience.

What sets BRICS apart is its ability to harmonize diverse political ideologies and economic systems under a unified framework of cooperation. The bloc's member states range from democracies like India and South Africa to state-driven economies like China and Russia, yet they converge on shared goals such as reducing global economic inequalities, enhancing regional connectivity, and championing a multipolar world order. Through its strategic initiatives and principled approach, BRICS has cemented itself as a formidable coalition advocating for a more just and equitable global system.

BRICS+ is an informal expansion of the core BRICS group to include new members and partnerships, reflecting its growing ambition to become a truly global platform for emerging economies. As of 2024, BRICS+ includes **Iran, Egypt, Ethiopia, and the United Arab Emirates**, alongside the original five BRICS members. This expansion was driven by the bloc's intention to create a broader coalition of nations to address shared challenges and amplify the voice of the Global South.

In January 2025, Indonesia officially became full member of BRICS bloc. The announcement was made by Brazil, the holder of the rotating presidency for 2025. The Brazilian government welcomed Indonesia's entry into the BRICS in a statement: "*With the largest population and economy in Southeast Asia, Indonesia shares with other members a commitment to reforming global governance institutions and contributes positively to deepening south-south cooperation*".

This historical trajectory not only underscores the bloc's growing influence but also highlights its unique role in reshaping global power dynamics. BRICS, from its inception, has been more than a coalition—it is a vision for a future where emerging economies wield greater influence in shaping the rules of the global economy.

BRICS principles

The principles of BRICS as articulated during the 2009 Yekaterinburg summit emphasized several key values that served as the foundation for the bloc's cooperative framework:

Sovereignty and Non-Interference: The summit underlined the importance of sovereignty, reinforcing that member states retain full control over their political, economic, and cultural systems without external interference. The principle of non-interference was closely tied to this, ensuring that the bloc would respect the internal affairs of each member nation.

Equality: Despite differences in economic size and global influence among the founding members—Brazil, Russia, India, and China—the principle of equality was emphasized. All members were accorded an equal voice in discussions and decision-making, ensuring a collaborative and non-hierarchical approach to addressing global challenges.

Mutual Respect and Benefit: Recognizing the diversity of political and economic systems within the group, the bloc emphasized mutual respect as a cornerstone of cooperation. Mutual benefit underscored the aim of creating win-win partnerships, particularly in trade, investment, and financial collaboration.

Commitment to Multilateralism: The leaders reaffirmed their commitment to a multilateral world order where global decisions are made through inclusive and representative international institutions rather than being dictated by a few dominant powers. This included calls for reforms in the IMF and World Bank to better reflect the realities of the 21st century.

Sustainable Development and Global Stability: The summit emphasized the need for sustainable development and global stability. This included addressing issues like food security, climate change, and trade imbalances, while also aiming to create a more predictable and stable financial environment by advocating for a diversified global reserve currency system.

Strengthening Cooperation among Emerging Economies: BRICS aimed to deepen collaboration in areas such as trade, investment, and knowledge-sharing among its members. This cooperation was seen as critical to reducing the vulnerabilities of emerging economies in a global system heavily influenced by developed nations.

These principles, articulated during the first summit, have continued to guide the bloc's initiatives and its evolving role as a counterweight to Western-centric global institutions. They remain central to the cooperative framework of BRICS, fostering solidarity among its members while advocating for a more equitable global order.

Economic Might: The Global Reach of BRICS+

BRICS+, as of 2024, has solidified itself as a transformative force on the global stage, reflecting the growing significance of emerging economies in reshaping the international economic and political order. This expanded coalition of nine nations—Brazil, Russia, India, China, South Africa, Iran, Egypt, Ethiopia, and the United Arab Emirates (UAE)—represents 44% of the world's population and commands nearly 37% of global GDP measured by purchasing power parity (PPP). The bloc's reach and influence transcend borders, uniting nations from diverse regions to collectively address the most pressing challenges of our time.

Unmatched Collective Influence

The economic weight of BRICS+ is immense, with its member states collectively controlling 42% of global foreign exchange (FX) reserves. This financial clout has positioned the bloc as a major stakeholder in international finance, offering an alternative narrative to the dominance of Western-led financial institutions. By leveraging their reserves and financial institutions such as the New Development Bank (NDB), BRICS+ nations are actively pursuing initiatives aimed at reducing their reliance on the

US dollar—a cornerstone of their de-dollarization strategy.

The group's influence is equally pronounced in natural resource management. Together, BRICS+ nations are custodians of vast reserves of critical resources, including energy, minerals, and agricultural commodities. These resources not only underpin their domestic economies but also provide them with leverage in international trade and negotiations.

China: The Economic Powerhouse

China, the world's second-largest economy, is the cornerstone of BRICS+, contributing over 52% of the bloc's GDP. With its robust manufacturing base, advanced technological capabilities, and expansive Belt and Road Initiative (BRI), China plays a pivotal role in shaping the group's economic strategies. Its influence extends beyond economics, as it serves as a key driver of BRICS+ initiatives in infrastructure development, renewable energy, and regional connectivity.

Diversity in Economic Strength and Perspectives

While China's dominance is undeniable, the inclusion of smaller economies like Ethiopia and the UAE adds depth and diversity to BRICS+. Ethiopia, with its growing population and strategic location in Africa, brings a unique perspective on development challenges and opportunities in the Global South. The UAE, on the other hand, contributes its expertise in global trade, energy markets, and financial services, underscoring the bloc's commitment to fostering partnerships that bridge regions and industries.

This diversity is one of BRICS+'s greatest strengths. The unique capabilities and resources of each member state enable the bloc to address a wide array of challenges, from food security to energy transitions, in a holistic manner. For instance, Brazil's agricultural expertise, Russia's energy dominance, India's technological prowess, and South Africa's mineral wealth combine to create a multidimensional approach to economic development and global problem-solving.

A Dominant Force in Global Commodity Markets

BRICS+ is a powerhouse in commodity markets, collectively accounting for 37% of the global fuel trade. This dominance is particularly significant in an era of energy transitions, as BRICS+ nations not only supply but also consume a substantial portion of the world's energy resources. Russia and the UAE, as major oil and gas exporters, complement the energy needs of industrial powerhouses like China and India. This synergy has the potential to transform energy markets, especially as the bloc explores alternative trade arrangements and renewable energy collaborations.

Beyond energy, BRICS+ nations are major players in agricultural commodities, metals, and rare earth minerals, which are critical for technologies such as electric vehicles and renewable energy systems. These resources enhance the bloc's bargaining power in global trade negotiations and reinforce its economic resilience.

A Work in Progress

Despite its impressive achievements, BRICS+ remains a work in progress. The bloc faces challenges in integrating its diverse economies and aligning the varied political priorities of its member states. Structural differences between highly industrialized nations like China and resource-dependent economies like Ethiopia require careful navigation to ensure equitable development and decision-making within the group.

The bloc's true potential lies in harnessing synergies between its members. By fostering deeper economic and political integration, BRICS+ can create a robust framework for addressing shared challenges such as climate change, infrastructure deficits, and trade imbalances. Initiatives such as the BRICS+ payment system, which seeks to reduce reliance on Western financial systems, are examples of the innovative solutions that the bloc can pioneer.

BRICS+, with its vast resources, financial strength, and diversity, is poised to play a transformative role in shaping the future of global governance. While its path is not without challenges, the bloc's commitment to inclusivity, sustainability, and multipolarity ensures that it remains a formidable force in the evolving global landscape.

The Expanding Horizon of BRICS Membership: A Growing Global Appeal

As the influence of BRICS rises, the allure of joining this dynamic coalition has become irresistible for nations seeking to amplify their voice in the global arena. By 2024, the group has grown to nine members, and its gravitational pull continues to attract suitors from every corner of the globe. With its promise of fostering a multipolar world order, BRICS has emerged as a magnet for nations eager to challenge Western-dominated financial and governance systems.

New Entrants and Interested Nations

A wave of countries has either formally applied or expressed an intent to join, painting a picture of BRICS as the leading alternative alliance for emerging economies.

SaudiArabia: The kingdom, a titan in global energy markets, has shown significant interest. Invited during the 2023 BRICS summit, its potential membership would elevate BRICS+'s energy dominance to nearly half of global oil production, solidifying its role in global energy security.

Argentina: Initially a strong candidate under President Alberto Fernández, Argentina's enthusiasm waned with the election of Javier Milei, who pivoted the country's foreign policy. While the nation ultimately withdrew, its earlier interest signals the bloc's appeal to major South American economies.

Turkey: Positioned at the crossroads of Europe and Asia, Turkey formally submitted its application in 2024. With its dual identity as a NATO member and an EU aspirant, Turkey's entry would symbolize a significant bridge between East and West.

Pakistan: Despite challenges posed by its complex relationship with India, Pakistan expressed interest in joining BRICS, emphasizing the bloc's reputation as a counterbalance to Western alliances.

Senegal, Sri Lanka, and Algeria: These nations submitted applications in 2023 and 2024, highlighting the growing interest from regions such as Africa and South Asia. Although Algeria later withdrew its application, the interest from these countries showcases the bloc's widening appeal.

Observers and Future Candidates: Nations like **Indonesia, Malaysia, Bangladesh, Thailand**, and **Nigeria** have participated in BRICS+ dialogues or shown interest in aligning with the group's goals, hinting at the bloc's future expansion into Southeast Asia and deeper into Africa.

What Does This Mean for Economic Size and Power?

The inclusion of potential new members would:

- Expand the bloc's energy dominance, particularly if **Saudi Arabia** joins, elevating its share of global oil production from 30% to 41%.
- Deepen its representation of the Global South, bringing diverse economies with untapped potential into a unified framework.
- Increase its role in global trade flows, with members contributing to critical supply chains in commodities, technology, and energy.

A Force for Change

The growing list of applicants signals more than just expanding numbers. It represents a shift in global dynamics—a movement toward a multipolar order where emerging economies shape the narrative. BRICS' expanded influence challenges the dominance of Western-centric institutions, offering a more inclusive platform for collaboration.

As more nations look to join, BRICS+ is not just a coalition; it is becoming a transformative global force, redefining the economic and geopolitical landscape. With every new member, its economic size and power grow, enhancing its potential to lead the way toward a fairer, more balanced global order.

Milestones: Year-by-Year Decisions That Shaped BRICS

BRICS has been a trailblazer for global economic and political collaboration since its formal establishment in 2009. Through its annual summits, the bloc has consistently tackled critical global issues, setting milestones that highlight its evolving role in reshaping the international order.

2009: Inaugural Summit and the Call for a Multipolar Financial System

The first BRICS summit, held in **Yekaterinburg, Russia** on June 16, 2009, was convened amidst the global financial crisis. Leaders of Brazil, Russia, India, and China issued a call for a more inclusive and representative financial system, emphasizing the need for a **"diverse, stable, and predictable" global reserve currency**. This was seen as an implicit critique of the US dollar's dominance. Discussions at the summit focused on global economic stability, food and energy security, and reforming international financial institutions like the IMF to reflect the growing influence of emerging markets.

2014: Fortaleza Summit – The Birth of BRICS Financial Institutions

The **6th BRICS Summit in Fortaleza, Brazil**, marked a turning point in the bloc's history with the establishment of two key financial mechanisms:

- The **New Development Bank (NDB)**, a multilateral financial institution, was created to finance infrastructure and sustainable development projects in BRICS and other emerging economies. Each member initially contributed $10 billion to the bank, highlighting its equal governance structure.
- The **Contingent Reserve Arrangement (CRA)** was established as a $100 billion currency pool to provide liquidity support during balance of payments crises. These initiatives signalled BRICS' commitment to self-reliance and financial resilience.

2015: Push for a BRICS Payment System

At the **7th BRICS Summit in Ufa, Russia**, discussions began on creating a BRICS payment system to reduce reliance on the Western-dominated SWIFT network. Proposals included settlement in local currencies to enhance financial independence. This initiative laid the groundwork for the ongoing exploration of alternatives like BRICS Pay and digital currencies.

2021: Conceptualizing a BRICS Basket Reserve Currency

The **13th BRICS Summit**, held virtually and hosted by India, saw the announcement of a **basket reserve currency** combining BRICS nations' currencies, backed by precious metals. This initiative aimed to challenge the dominance of the US dollar in global trade while ensuring stability and predictability in financial transactions.

2024: Expansion and Digital Innovations

The **16th BRICS Summit**, held in Kazan, Russia, in October 2024, was a landmark event that showcased the bloc's expanded ambitions, strengthened collaboration, and enhanced global influence. Under the theme **"Strengthening Multilateralism for Just Global Development and Security"**, this summit marked several key decisions that aim to shape the economic and strategic future of the bloc and its new members.

Advancing the BRICS Payment System

A significant focus of the summit was the **BRICS Cross-Border Payments Initiative (BCBPI)**. Recognizing the inefficiencies and risks posed by dependence on Western-dominated payment systems like SWIFT, the leaders endorsed discussions on a **dedicated BRICS payment mechanism**. Key aspects included:

- **Encouraging local currency settlements**: This would reduce the reliance on the US dollar, foster financial independence, and lower transaction costs among BRICS+ nations.

- **Exploring cross-border settlement infrastructure**: The summit proposed creating an independent system, tentatively named **BRICS Clear**, to streamline transactions between members and complement existing financial networks.
- **Feasibility studies on digital currencies**: Building on past discussions, the leaders encouraged exploration of central bank digital currencies (CBDCs) and how they could integrate with the BCBPI.

These measures aim to provide a resilient, low-cost alternative to existing systems, aligning with BRICS' broader goal of enhancing economic sovereignty and connectivity among members.

Strengthening Digital Trade Frameworks

Digital trade was highlighted as a critical driver of economic growth and innovation. The summit acknowledged the transformative potential of e-commerce for small and medium enterprises (SMEs) in emerging markets and emphasized:

- **Consumer rights and trust**: Cooperation on policies to enhance the security of e-commerce transactions and address online dispute resolutions.

- **Support for small-value product trade**: This initiative targets the inclusion of small businesses in cross-border markets, leveraging e-commerce to access global buyers.
- **Governance of cross-border data flows**: The leaders called for fair, inclusive frameworks for data governance, enabling developing nations to benefit from the burgeoning digital economy and emerging technologies like artificial intelligence.

By advancing these frameworks, BRICS aims to create an inclusive digital ecosystem that supports innovation and equitable access for its members and partners.

Establishing the BRICS Grain Exchange

Amid rising concerns over global food security, the summit took decisive steps to create the **BRICS Grain Exchange**. This platform is designed to:

- **Facilitate agricultural trade**: By streamlining the exchange of commodities, the Grain Exchange ensures stable and transparent food trade within the bloc.
- **Support smallholder farmers**: With a focus on sustainable practices, the initiative aims to integrate low-income and resource-poor farmers into global supply chains.

- **Promote fair trade**: The platform aligns with the bloc's commitment to rules-based agricultural trade that is free from restrictive economic measures inconsistent with WTO rules.

This exchange is envisioned as the first step toward broader integration of agricultural sectors across BRICS+, enhancing food security and fostering resilience against supply chain disruptions.

Recurring Themes and Global Relevance

Each summit has served as a platform for BRICS nations to address global challenges, from climate change to technological innovation. The bloc has consistently called for:

- Greater representation of emerging economies in global governance institutions like the UN Security Council and IMF.
- Collaboration on cutting-edge technologies, particularly in renewable energy, artificial intelligence, and space exploration.

By evolving its agenda and institutions, BRICS has cemented itself as a counterweight to the traditional global order, championing a vision of inclusive growth and multipolarity. These milestones underscore the bloc's commitment to fostering economic resilience, innovation, and sustainable development in an ever-changing world.

Dedollarization and the Bridge to Economic Sovereignty

At the core of BRICS+ lies an ambitious agenda that seeks to challenge the long-standing dominance of the US dollar in global trade and finance. This process of **de-dollarization** is more than a symbolic gesture; it is a deliberate and strategic effort to empower member states with greater financial autonomy, reduce vulnerability to external economic shocks, and forge a more equitable global financial system.

The Motivation Behind De-dollarization

The US dollar's dominant role in international trade and as a global reserve currency has historically provided the United States with significant economic and geopolitical leverage. For BRICS+ nations, this reliance on the dollar translates into exposure to economic risks, including fluctuating exchange rates and the impact of US monetary policy on their economies. Moreover, the weaponization of the dollar through sanctions and trade restrictions has further reinforced the need for an alternative system that safeguards the economic sovereignty of emerging markets

.

Gold as a Stable Reserve Asset

One key strategy in this transition is the accumulation of gold reserves. BRICS+ countries have been steadily increasing their gold holdings as part of their foreign exchange reserves. Gold is viewed as a stable asset that provides protection against currency volatility and external pressures. For instance:

- Between 2008 and 2021, BRICS+ nations collectively acquired more than 6,600 tons of gold, raising their share of global gold reserves significantly.
- While gold currently constitutes approximately 10% of BRICS+ central bank reserves, compared to the global average of 20%, there remains significant potential for growth in this area, further enhancing the bloc's financial independence.

The Proposed BRICS Payment System

Central to the de-dollarization agenda is the development of a **BRICS payment system** that reduces reliance on traditional dollar-based financial networks such as SWIFT. The proposed system aims to:

- Enable cross-border transactions in local currencies, bypassing the dollar as an intermediary.
- Increase financial efficiency by lowering transaction costs and reducing delays in international trade settlements.
- Provide a secure and resilient alternative that shields member states from economic sanctions and geopolitical pressures.

This payment system is complemented by initiatives to integrate digital currencies, including the exploration of central bank digital currencies (CBDCs). These innovations could potentially revolutionize cross-border transactions, offering faster, more transparent, and decentralized payment solutions.

Challenges to a Unified BRICS Currency

While the idea of a unified BRICS currency has been floated, it remains a long-term goal due to several logistical and geopolitical challenges:

- **Diverse Economies**: The vast differences in economic size, structure, and monetary policy among BRICS+ members make it difficult to establish a single currency.
- **Geopolitical Dynamics**: Political tensions and differing strategic priorities among member states may hinder consensus on such an initiative.
- **Technical and Institutional Gaps**: Developing the necessary financial infrastructure and regulatory frameworks for a shared currency requires significant investment and coordination.

Progress in Bilateral and Regional Currency Use

Despite the hurdles, incremental progress is already evident in the increased use of local currencies in trade:

- The **Chinese yuan** has become a key currency in trade between China and Russia, with significant increases in yuan-denominated transactions in recent years.

- India and Russia have also adopted mechanisms to settle trade in rupees and rubles for energy imports and exports, further reducing dependency on the dollar.

A Vision for Financial Sovereignty

The dedollarization efforts of BRICS+ are about more than reducing reliance on the US dollar—they symbolize the bloc's vision for a more equitable global financial system. By promoting the use of local currencies, building gold reserves, and developing innovative payment systems, BRICS+ aims to empower its members with greater economic resilience and sovereignty. While a unified currency may still be a distant goal, the bloc's incremental steps are paving the way for a future where emerging economies hold greater control over their financial destinies.

As BRICS+ continues to advance its dedollarization agenda, it not only strengthens the economic foundations of its member states but also challenges the traditional paradigms of global finance, fostering a multipolar world order.

Opportunities in Investment and Growth

BRICS+ presents a transformative platform for global economic collaboration, unlocking vast opportunities for investment and growth across its diverse member states. From infrastructure development to renewable energy, and enhanced trade facilitation, the bloc is poised to be a magnet for businesses, investors, and innovators.

Infrastructure Development: Building the Foundations of Growth

The **New Development Bank (NDB)**, a cornerstone of BRICS' financial architecture, has played a transformative role in funding projects that align with the bloc's vision for sustainable development and economic resilience. Since its inception, the NDB has approved numerous projects across renewable energy, transportation, and digital infrastructure, channeling billions of dollars into initiatives that address pressing developmental needs.

Renewable Energy Projects

The NDB has prioritized investments in renewable energy, reflecting BRICS+'s commitment to combating climate change and fostering sustainable growth:

Investment Scale: As of 2024, the NDB has allocated over **$5 billion** to renewable energy projects across its member states. This includes funding for solar farms in India, wind energy in South Africa, and hydroelectric projects in Brazil.

Impact: These projects have contributed to expanding clean energy capacity and reducing carbon footprints, aligning with the bloc's climate commitments under the Paris Agreement.

Transportation Networks

Infrastructure development remains a pivotal focus for the NDB, particularly in enhancing connectivity and trade efficiency:

Project Highlights:

- High-speed rail systems in India aimed at reducing travel time and boosting regional trade.
- Port expansions in South Africa to facilitate greater trade volumes and enhance global competitiveness.

Financial Commitment: The NDB has financed transportation projects with an estimated value of **$7 billion**, emphasizing the importance of efficient logistics in fostering economic growth.

Digital Infrastructure

To bridge the digital divide and support emerging technologies, the NDB has invested in digital infrastructure projects that empower member states to integrate into the global digital economy:

- **Fiber-Optic Networks**: Significant funding has been allocated to extend high-speed internet access in rural areas across BRICS nations.

- **5G Deployment**: Support for the rollout of 5G technology in countries like China and Brazil has been a priority, enabling faster connectivity and innovation
- **Overall Contribution**: Digital infrastructure projects funded by the NDB amount to approximately **$3 billion**, enhancing both economic inclusivity and technological competitiveness.

The Strategic Role of the NDB

The NDB's targeted investments demonstrate its pivotal role in shaping the developmental trajectory of BRICS+ nations. By addressing gaps in renewable energy, transportation, and digital connectivity, the bank not only fosters economic growth but also reinforces the bloc's vision of a sustainable and interconnected future.

The continued expansion of the NDB's portfolio underscores its potential to drive transformative change across emerging markets, leveraging the collective strength of its member states to address global challenges.

These efforts not only create jobs but also pave the way for long-term economic growth by improving efficiency and reducing transaction costs.

Sustainable Energy: A Green Future

BRICS+ is at the forefront of the global transition to sustainable energy systems. Member nations are investing heavily in green technologies to reduce carbon emissions while meeting rising energy demands:

- **Solar and Wind Energy**: India and China lead in solar power installations, while South Africa is harnessing wind energy to address energy shortages.
- **Hydroelectric Projects**: Brazil's abundant rivers provide a natural advantage for hydropower, which continues to be a significant part of its energy mix.
- **Collaborative Energy Research**: The BRICS Energy Research Cooperation Platform fosters collaboration on cutting-edge renewable energy technologies and sustainable practices.

These initiatives not only contribute to global climate goals but also create investment opportunities in clean energy technologies and infrastructure.

Enhancing Intra-BRICS Trade: A Unified Market

One of the most significant opportunities within BRICS+ is the facilitation of intra-bloc trade, which offers immense growth potential:

- **Trade Agreements**: Simplified trade policies and reduced tariffs among members have made it easier for businesses to operate across borders, particularly in key sectors like agriculture, technology, and manufacturing.
- **BRICS Grain Exchange**: The establishment of this platform facilitates agricultural trade, ensuring food security while supporting smallholder farmers and creating lucrative opportunities for agribusinesses.
- **E-Commerce Expansion**: Digital trade frameworks are enabling small and medium enterprises (SMEs) to participate in global markets, fostering innovation and economic inclusivity.

Enhanced trade cooperation not only strengthens economic ties but also creates a resilient economic ecosystem less dependent on external influences.

Opportunities for Investors

The investment potential within BRICS+ is vast and varied:

Special Economic Zones (SEZs): Designed to attract foreign direct investment, SEZs within BRICS countries focus on high-tech manufacturing, IT services, tourism, and other growth industries.

Innovation Ecosystems: Platforms such as the BRICS Startup Forum foster entrepreneurship, offering opportunities to invest in disruptive technologies and scalable business models.

Financial Markets: With initiatives like the BRICS Payment System, investors can expect streamlined cross-border transactions and reduced reliance on traditional financial networks.

The vision of BRICS+ is not merely economic—it is transformative. By fostering investment in infrastructure, championing sustainable energy, and enhancing trade frameworks, the bloc creates unparalleled opportunities for growth. For businesses and investors alike, BRICS+ represents a gateway to the future—a future driven by innovation, inclusivity, and shared prosperity.

Challenges: The Roadblocks to Unity

While BRICS+ has emerged as a transformative force in global politics and economics, its journey is not without obstacles. The diversity that enriches the bloc also brings challenges, with differences in geopolitics, economics, and institutional capacities often complicating its path to unity. These challenges test the resilience of BRICS+ as it seeks to redefine global governance.

Geopolitical Tensions: Balancing Divergent Aspirations

The BRICS+ bloc is a tapestry of nations with distinct histories, ambitions, and regional priorities. While all members share the goal of a multipolar world order, their specific interests can clash:

- **China's Expanding Influence**: As the economic giant of the group, China's Belt and Road Initiative and its strategic moves in Africa and South Asia often position it as a leader. However, this dominance can cause unease among other members, particularly India, which has its own regional ambitions and longstanding border disputes with China.
- **Regional Priorities**: Brazil's focus on South America, South Africa's leadership in Africa, and Russia's geopolitical maneuvering in Eastern Europe and Central Asia sometimes pull the bloc in different directions, making consensus on global issues challenging.
- **Bilateral Disputes**: Historical and current frictions, such as the India-China border tensions, highlight the difficulty of aligning national interests under a single cooperative framework.

Navigating these differences requires diplomacy, trust, and a shared commitment to the bloc's overarching vision.

Economic Disparities: Bridging the Gap

The economic landscape of BRICS+ is as varied as its geography. While China and India are global powerhouses, smaller economies like Ethiopia and South

Africa struggle with development challenges. This disparity creates an uneven playing field:

- **China's Economic Weight**: Contributing over half of BRICS+ GDP, China's dominance risks overshadowing the voices of smaller members, potentially creating a perception of inequality.
- **Varied Development Goals**: The priorities of resource-dependent economies like Ethiopia differ significantly from the technological ambitions of India or the industrial strategies of Russia. Aligning these divergent economic goals remains a persistent challenge.
- **Access to Resources**: Smaller members often lack the financial and institutional capacity to fully engage in BRICS+ initiatives, widening the gap between the bloc's largest and smallest economies.

Fostering equitable participation and ensuring that all members benefit from the bloc's initiatives is essential for long-term cohesion.

Institutional Development: Building Strong Foundations

The ambitions of BRICS+ demand robust institutions capable of executing complex initiatives. Yet, the bloc's institutional frameworks are still evolving:

- **Coordination Challenges**: Developing streamlined processes for decision-making across diverse political systems is a complex task, leading to delays in implementing projects like the BRICS payment system.
- **Capacity Gaps**: While nations like China and India possess advanced infrastructure and expertise, others face limitations in institutional capacity, creating disparities in engagement.
- **Governance and Accountability**: As the bloc expands, ensuring transparency and equal representation in governance structures is critical to maintaining trust among members.

Investing in institutional strength will be key to transforming the bloc's ambitious visions into actionable outcomes.

External Resistance: A World Watching Warily

As BRICS+ grows in influence, it faces scrutiny and opposition from Western powers, which often perceive the bloc as a challenger to their dominance:

- **Economic Containment**: Trade alliances and agreements led by Western nations often exclude BRICS members, limiting their access to key markets and resources.
- **Sanctions and Restrictions**: Countries like Russia and Iran face economic sanctions, which

complicate their integration into global financial systems and impact BRICS+ projects.

- **Narrative and Perception**: Western media and policymakers often frame BRICS+ as a geopolitical disruptor, creating barriers to its global acceptance and cooperation with non-member states.

Overcoming this resistance requires strategic communication and forging partnerships that highlight the bloc's commitment to inclusivity and development.

Expansion Complexities: Growing Pains

The inclusion of new members like Iran, Egypt, Ethiopia, and the UAE has brought fresh perspectives and resources, but it also adds layers of complexity:

- **Diverse Perspectives**: Each new member brings unique priorities and challenges, which can complicate decision-making and dilute the bloc's focus.
- **Integration Costs**: Expanding membership demands adjustments to governance structures and financial contributions, placing additional strain on the bloc's resources.
- **Maintaining Cohesion**: Balancing the interests of a larger and more diverse membership is a delicate task that requires consensus-building and shared vision.

Managing these complexities is crucial to ensuring that expansion strengthens rather than fragments the bloc.

A Future Beyond Challenges

While BRICS+ faces significant hurdles, its diversity is also its strength. The bloc's ability to unite countries across regions, cultures, and economic systems is a testament to its potential. By addressing these challenges with innovation and cooperation, BRICS+ can transform obstacles into opportunities and fulfill its vision of a fairer, more balanced global order.

The road ahead will not be easy, but with determination, diplomacy, and shared purpose, BRICS+ can emerge stronger and more unified, ready to lead the world toward a multipolar future.

Chapter conclusion: A Force for a Multipolar World

BRICS+ represents more than an economic coalition; it embodies the collective aspirations of emerging markets striving for equity, sovereignty, and resilience in a rapidly evolving global order. From its inception as a concept in 2001 to its transformation into a powerful bloc and expanded platform by 2024, BRICS+ has proven its ability to challenge traditional paradigms and offer innovative solutions for the challenges of our time.

The bloc's journey has been marked by groundbreaking milestones: the establishment of the New Development Bank, the creation of the Contingent Reserve Arrangement, and bold steps toward dedollarization and the use of digital currencies. BRICS+ has also laid a foundation for inclusive growth by addressing issues ranging from infrastructure deficits to climate change, and from digital connectivity to trade integration. Its ability to harmonize diverse political ideologies and economic systems into a unified framework underscores its strength and potential.

Yet, the path forward is not without obstacles. Geopolitical tensions, economic disparities, institutional gaps, and external resistance test the cohesion and ambition of BRICS+. Nevertheless, these challenges also serve as catalysts for innovation and deeper collaboration. The bloc's commitment to inclusivity and sustainability, combined with its expanding influence, demonstrates that it is well-positioned to address the complexities of a multipolar world.

The potential of BRICS+ lies in its diversity and shared purpose. By fostering a sense of mutual benefit and collaboration, the bloc has set the stage for transformative change—not just for its members, but for the global community. Its efforts to create a more equitable and balanced international system reflect the hopes of nations seeking an alternative to the status quo.

As BRICS+ continues to evolve, it stands as a symbol of possibility—a beacon for countries aspiring to forge a future where development is not defined by exclusion or dominance, but by partnership and shared progress. The bloc's vision is clear: a global order that respects diversity, promotes sustainable development, and amplifies the voices of those long overlooked in the corridors of power. In this vision, BRICS+ has not only become a powerful force in global governance but also a harbinger of a more just and prosperous world.

Chapter (2)

Brazil: A Green and Digital Economy on the Rise

"The Global Alliance against Hunger and Poverty is already in an advanced stage of membership"

Luiz Inácio Lula da Silva, President of Brazil

Brazil, the largest and most populous country in South America, occupies a commanding position in the eastern part of the continent, bordering the Atlantic Ocean. Covering an area of over 8.5 million square kilometers—slightly smaller than the United States—it boasts diverse terrains, from the vast Amazon Basin and the Pantanal wetlands to rolling lowlands and coastal mountain ranges. Its geographical boundaries stretch across ten countries, including Argentina, Bolivia, and Venezuela, with a coastline of 7,491 kilometers, making it a vital player in regional trade and maritime activities.

The nation's population, exceeding 220 million, is predominantly concentrated along the southeastern coastline in urban centers such as São Paulo, Rio de Janeiro, and Brasília. Urbanization has reached 87.8%, reflecting a sophisticated infrastructure network and urban-based economic activities. With a median age of 35 years, Brazil benefits from a relatively young and active labor force, though it is already witnessing the early phases of demographic transition with a growing elderly population.

Economically, Brazil ranks as one of the world's largest emerging markets, driven by robust industries in agriculture, hydropower, and natural resource extraction. Its rich reserves of iron ore, petroleum, and rare earth elements, combined with a strong emphasis on green technologies and innovative financial systems like the PIX instant payment platform, underscore its competitive advantage. The government's commitment to halving deforestation in the Amazon and implementing a mandatory carbon market system further reflects its ecological priorities.

Brazil's economic view in 2024 shines with resilience and innovation, thanks to strategic fiscal policies, a green-focused agenda, and digital transformation. Brazil's commitment to sustainable and inclusive growth is clear, which positions the nation as an attractive destination for investors targeting green projects and fintech. This chapter highlights Brazil's remarkable geographical and demographic features alongside its economic strengths.

Economic Vitality: Solid Growth and Inflation on a Steady Decline

Brazil has displayed remarkable resilience in navigating a complex global economic environment, achieving consistent economic expansion. In 2023, the nation's GDP grew by 2.9%, surpassing expectations due to record agricultural and hydrocarbon production. Brazil's role as a leading exporter of soybeans, iron ore, and oil underpins its economic stability, while a robust services sector and strong household consumption provided additional momentum. Although GDP growth was projected to moderate to 2.1% in 2024, influenced by restrictive monetary policies aimed at curbing inflation, the medium-term outlook remains optimistic.

Nominal GDP and PPP GDP for Brazil

Based on the data from the IMF and other authoritative sources:

Nominal GDP in 2022 was at USD 2.0 trillion, and grew up in 2023 to USD 2.17 trillion, and projected to grow up to USD 2.24 trillion and USD 2.36 trillion in 2024 and 2025 respectively. The GDP at Purchasing Power Parity (PPP) in 2022 was therefore at USD 3.87 trillion and grew up in 2023 to USD 4.03 trillion and projected at USD 4.18 trillion and USD 4.32 trillion in FY24 and FY25 respectively

The future trajectory anticipates stable growth in both nominal GDP and GDP at PPP, driven by structural reforms, green initiatives, and improvements in productivity

Structural reforms, such as the implementation of the VAT overhaul, are expected to enhance productivity and tax equity, contributing to growth projections of 2.5% by 2027. This outlook is further bolstered by Brazil's growing investments in renewable energy and green technologies, which align with global shifts toward sustainability.

Inflation Control: A Testament to Monetary Discipline

Inflation management remains a cornerstone of Brazil's economic strategy. The Central Bank of Brazil (BCB) has executed a calibrated approach to monetary policy, significantly reducing inflation from its 2022 peak of 12.1%. By May 2024, inflation had dropped to 3.9%, comfortably within the target tolerance range. This achievement reflects effective communication, a measured pace of interest rate adjustments, and a steadfast commitment to the 3% inflation target, set to be achieved by 2026. These efforts are further supported by Brazil's proactive fiscal policies, which aim to reduce the public debt burden while preserving space for critical investments. Such stability reassures investors, businesses, and households, creating a conducive environment for long-term economic confidence.

Labor Market Strength: A Resilient Workforce and Rising Incomes

Brazil's labor market has shown notable improvements, with unemployment declining to 7.5% in early 2024, the lowest rate in a decade. Job creation has been robust across major demographic groups, particularly benefiting young workers and those with lower levels of formal education. Real wages have also rebounded, boosting household purchasing power and stimulating private consumption. Programs like "Desenrola," which support low-income households in restructuring their debt, have further strengthened financial inclusion and consumer confidence. The expansion of formal employment opportunities has reduced economic vulnerabilities while reinforcing the domestic demand that drives key industries such as retail, construction, and services. This strong labor market performance positions Brazil as a stable and appealing destination for both domestic and foreign investments.

Broader Implications

Brazil's economic achievements are a testament to its ability to adapt to challenges while advancing structural reforms and fostering sustainable growth. By controlling inflation, maintaining a strong labor market, and prioritizing inclusive policies, Brazil continues to enhance its appeal as a hub for investment, innovation, and development.

Fiscal Fortitude: Balancing Public Spending with Debt Control

Brazil has taken deliberate steps to reconcile the dual imperatives of public investment and debt sustainability, charting a clear path toward fiscal health. The federal government aimed to significantly reduce its primary deficit from 2.4% of GDP in 2023 to 0.6% in 2024, underpinned by a comprehensive fiscal framework designed to enhance revenue generation and rationalize expenditures. By 2029, Brazil is projected to achieve a primary surplus of 1% of GDP, reflecting its commitment to fiscal discipline while fostering conditions for long-term economic growth. These efforts are particularly critical as the nation addresses structural challenges such as elevated public debt and persistent demands for infrastructure and social investments.

Deficit Reduction Path: Combining Revenue Growth and Strategic Spending

A cornerstone of Brazil's fiscal strategy is its emphasis on revenue growth through tax reforms and improved collection mechanisms. The landmark VAT reform of 2023 represents a transformative step, harmonizing Brazil's fragmented federal and subnational VAT systems. This streamlining is expected to not only improve compliance and reduce tax evasion but also boost productivity by simplifying the business environment.

Simultaneously, the government has adopted a new fiscal rule that balances spending discipline with flexibility. This rule allows expenditure growth between 0.6% and 2.5% annually, contingent on revenue performance and primary balance targets. This approach enables the government to prioritize essential sectors such as health, education, and infrastructure, ensuring that fiscal consolidation does not come at the expense of critical public services. The rule also includes provisions for transparency and accountability, further strengthening fiscal governance.

Fiscal Policy Innovations: A Foundation for Stability and Growth

Brazil's fiscal journey over the past few years reflects a nation striving to balance short-term challenges with long-term sustainability. As the largest economy in South America, Brazil's fiscal policy aims to address social demands while keeping debt and inflation under control. Here's how the country is navigating its fiscal position and trajectory:

The Fiscal Deficit: A Journey Toward Balance

In 2022, Brazil's fiscal position showed resilience with a federal primary surplus of **0.5% of GDP**, signaling a rebound after pandemic-era spending. However, the landscape shifted in 2023, with a **2.4% primary deficit** emerging as the government prioritized social programs, including expanded benefits under Bolsa Família, and resolved long-standing liabilities, such as judicial claims ("precatórios").

The deficit trajectory takes a decisive turn in 2024, with the government aim to narrow it to **0.6% of GDP**. This ambitious reduction is bolstered by:

- A **landmark VAT reform**, harmonizing federal and state tax structures.
- Moderation in fiscal stimulus measures as economic growth stabilizes.
- Stronger adherence to the new **fiscal rule**, which ties spending growth to revenue performance.

Looking further ahead, Brazil plans to transition to a **primary surplus of 1% of GDP by 2029**, creating fiscal space for development priorities while managing its debt burden.

Public Debt: Stabilizing the Weight of Borrowing

Brazil's debt levels remain a critical factor in its fiscal planning.

- In 2022, net public debt stood at **56.1% of GDP**, while gross debt was significantly higher at **83.9% of GDP**.
- By 2023, net debt rose to **60.9% of GDP**, reflecting increased fiscal spending, while gross debt climbed to **84.7%**.

The outlook shows a stabilization of gross debt around **95% of GDP by 2029**, contingent on sustained revenue growth, controlled spending, and consistent economic expansion. However, **net debt** is expected to rise gradually, peaking at **71.8% of GDP by 2029**, driven by financing needs and the ongoing burden of interest payments.

Revenue and Spending: Engines of Fiscal Reform

At the heart of Brazil's fiscal strategy are structural reforms aimed at boosting revenues and improving the efficiency of public expenditures:

Revenue Growth Through Reform

- The **2023 VAT reform**, a game-changer for Brazil's complex tax system, seeks to streamline collection and boost productivity across sectors.
- Broadening the tax base by reducing inefficiencies and addressing tax expenditures is expected to generate significant additional revenue.

Spending Discipline Under the Fiscal Rule

- Brazil's new fiscal rule, approved in 2023, ensures spending growth is tightly linked to revenue performance. Annual expenditure increases are capped between 0.6% and 2.5%, allowing the government to prioritize essential investments without overburdening public finances.

- Efficiency improvements in social programs, such as Bolsa Família, are enabling resources to reach those most in need while minimizing waste.

Inflation and Interest: The Balancing Act

Inflation and interest payments present both a challenge and an opportunity for fiscal management.

- Inflation, which reached **12.1% in 2022**, has been brought under control, with projections suggesting it will stabilize at **3% by 2026**. This progress aligns with Brazil's monetary policy goals and enhances fiscal credibility.
- Interest payments, however, remain a heavy fiscal load, accounting for over **6% of GDP in 2023**. While this constrains public investment, the gradual stabilization of debt and inflation should reduce borrowing costs over time.

Risks and Resilience: Navigating the Uncertainties

Despite Brazil's robust fiscal strategy, challenges remain.

- The effectiveness of revenue reforms and fiscal discipline will be key to achieving the projected debt stabilization.

- Brazil's reliance on commodity exports makes it vulnerable to global price fluctuations, particularly for oil and soybeans.
- External risks, including global financial volatility and economic slowdowns in key trading partners like China and the US, could also impact revenue and growth prospects.

However, Brazil's resilience is reinforced by its sound foreign exchange reserves, flexible monetary policy, and government commitment to fiscal sustainability.

A Path Toward Stability

Brazil's fiscal trajectory highlights its determination to balance social development with financial discipline. As the government pursues reforms to expand revenue, control spending, and manage debt, the nation is positioning itself as a model of fiscal prudence in an emerging market context. Investors and stakeholders can look to Brazil's commitment to long-term stability as a foundation for sustained growth and resilience in the face of global challenges.

Strengthening Credibility and Economic Prospects

Brazil's fiscal reforms signify a decisive move toward securing its economic future. By enhancing revenue streams, prioritizing strategic investments, and maintaining strict control over debt accumulation, Brazil is poised to stabilize its debt-to-GDP ratio while creating room for growth-enhancing expenditures. These measures bolster Brazil's position as a regional leader in fiscal innovation and an attractive destination for long-term investment. The country's fiscal fortitude is a testament to its ability to adapt and thrive in a dynamic global economic landscape.

Investment Horizons: Green Transition, Fintech Expansion, and Digital Innovation

Brazil's dynamic green initiatives and innovative digital finance systems present an array of transformative investment opportunities. The nation's commitment to addressing environmental challenges, fostering technological advancements, and broadening access to finance underscores its dedication to sustainable and inclusive growth. With ambitious policies driving deforestation reduction, carbon market development, and fintech innovation, Brazil is paving the way for a modernized, green economy that attracts global investors.

Deforestation Reduction and Ecological Transformation

At the heart of Brazil's green strategy lies the **Ecological Transformation Plan**, which aims to halt illegal deforestation by 2030. In 2023, deforestation in the Amazon was reduced by an impressive 50%, resulting in an estimated 0.5-gigaton reduction in carbon emissions. This achievement is a cornerstone of Brazil's commitment to combating climate change, supported by increased funding for enforcement agencies like IBAMA. Investments in monitoring systems, stricter penalties for illegal activities, and community-based conservation programs have strengthened Brazil's capacity to preserve its vital ecosystems.

Brazil's **carbon market framework** further advances these goals. The introduction of a mandatory cap-and-trade system in 2023 has placed emission caps on companies releasing over 25,000 tons of CO2 annually, covering approximately 5,000 entities. This framework, complemented by the voluntary carbon market, allows credits from forest conservation projects to be traded internationally. The resulting investment influx is transforming Brazil's reforestation efforts and expanding opportunities in carbon offset projects, drawing interest from multinational corporations and green funds.

Green Bond Issuances and Renewable Energy Development

Brazil's financial sector has taken bold steps to integrate sustainability, beginning with the launch of its **first green and social sovereign bond** in 2023. The issuance, which established a benchmark for green finance in Brazil, provides a yield curve that bolsters investment in renewable energy, sustainable infrastructure, and social projects. A follow-up bond issuance is planned, reinforcing Brazil's role as a global leader in green finance.

To further capitalize on these opportunities, the **ECO Invest Brasil** program, initiated by the Ministry of Finance, mobilizes foreign capital for green infrastructure projects while offering FX hedging solutions to mitigate currency risk. This initiative enhances Brazil's attractiveness to international investors, particularly in renewable energy sectors such as solar, wind, and biofuels, where the country has abundant natural resources and technical expertise.

Fintech Expansion and Digital Finance Revolution

Brazil is at the forefront of a digital finance revolution, driven by rapid advancements in fintech and a regulatory framework that encourages innovation. The success of **PIX**, Brazil's instant payment system, is a testament to this transformation. With widespread adoption, PIX has significantly increased financial inclusion, reducing transaction costs for businesses and consumers alike. Its open-access model has spurred competition in the banking sector, leading to innovative financial products tailored to previously underserved markets.

The government's proactive stance on fostering **financial technology** includes investments in blockchain, digital wallets, and regulatory sandboxes that allow startups to test new solutions in a controlled environment. These initiatives have positioned Brazil as a leader in Latin America's fintech sector, attracting venture capital and fostering partnerships between local innovators and global tech giants.

Driving Technological Innovation

Brazil's investment landscape is further enhanced by its focus on **technological innovation** in areas such as artificial intelligence (AI), clean energy technologies, and smart agriculture. Public and private initiatives have enabled the integration of AI into key sectors, improving efficiency and productivity, particularly in agribusiness, which benefits from AI-driven crop management solutions. Combined with advancements in digital infrastructure, these technologies are transforming Brazil's economy, fostering an environment where innovation and sustainability intersect.

Broader Implications for Investors

Brazil's integrated approach to green finance, fintech expansion, and technological innovation offers a diversified investment horizon. The combination of strong regulatory frameworks, natural resource wealth, and a skilled workforce ensures long-term growth potential. These strategic initiatives, coupled with Brazil's proactive leadership in global climate efforts, position the nation as a vibrant hub for sustainable development and digital transformation, presenting unparalleled opportunities for forward-looking investors.

Digital Finance Innovation: PIX and Drex Leading the Way

Brazil has emerged as a global leader in digital finance, driven by transformative initiatives like Pix and the forthcoming Drex digital currency. These innovations, spearheaded by the Central Bank of Brazil (BCB), have revolutionized financial inclusion and reshaped the landscape of financial services. By combining accessibility, security, and cutting-edge technology, Pix and Drex are positioning Brazil as a trailblazer in the digital economy.

Pix: Transforming Payments with Instantaneous Transactions

Introduced in 2020, **Pix** is Brazil's highly successful real-time payment system. Its adoption has been nothing short of remarkable, with over 25 million transactions processed daily. Designed to provide instant and free transfers between bank accounts at any time, Pix has addressed a critical gap in the financial system, making it accessible to individuals and small businesses across all socioeconomic levels.

One of Pix's most significant contributions has been its role in advancing **financial inclusion**. By eliminating the need for costly traditional banking services, Pix has empowered Brazil's unbanked and underbanked populations, enabling them to participate fully in the digital economy. Small businesses and informal workers have particularly benefited, using Pix to receive payments instantly without incurring high fees.

Pix has also fostered greater **transparency** and **competition** in the financial sector. Its open architecture encourages the participation of fintech startups and digital payment providers, leading to innovative financial solutions. Moreover, Pix's high adoption rates have propelled Brazil to surpass global averages in per capita digital transactions. Looking ahead, the Central Bank aims to enhance Pix's capabilities, including features like recurring automatic payments, cross-border transfers, and integration with Drex, although resource limitations have delayed some of these expansions.

Drex: A Visionary Central Bank Digital Currency (CBDC)

Set to launch in 2025, **Drex** represents Brazil's bold foray into central bank digital currencies (CBDCs). Unlike traditional payment systems, Drex will operate on a **tokenized blockchain infrastructure**, enabling secure, regulated, and scalable financial services. This innovation has the potential to transform how Brazilians interact with money and credit systems.

Drex's core focus is on fostering **financial inclusion and innovation**. By allowing digital assets, such as tokenized government bonds, to serve as collateral for credit, Drex aims to democratize access to financing. This feature is particularly impactful for smaller borrowers, who often struggle to secure credit in traditional markets. Additionally, the use of **smart contracts** will facilitate automated transactions, streamlining processes like lending and repayments.

The digital currency's design also emphasizes cross-border functionality, paving the way for seamless international transactions. As Brazil integrates Drex into its financial system, it is addressing challenges related to **privacy, governance, and cybersecurity** to ensure the platform is robust and scalable. These measures are essential to Drex's success, as the currency is positioned to serve as a model for other emerging markets exploring CBDCs.

Broader Impacts on Brazil's Financial Ecosystem

Pix and Drex together signify a transformative shift in Brazil's financial landscape. Pix has already revolutionized payment systems, making financial services accessible to millions. Drex, with its focus on tokenization and smart contract integration, promises to elevate Brazil's economy further by providing a cutting-edge platform for digital transactions and credit access.

These innovations not only strengthen financial inclusion but also position Brazil as a leader in digital finance globally. By creating a secure, inclusive, and forward-thinking financial ecosystem, Brazil continues to set new benchmarks for how emerging markets can embrace digital transformation to drive sustainable growth.

Managing Risks: A Pathway of Resilience Amid Global Challenges

Brazil's growth prospects remain robust, but the country must navigate a complex landscape of global and domestic risks. Strategic policymaking and economic resilience are vital as Brazil addresses uncertainties in trade, commodities, and fiscal challenges while leveraging its strengths to sustain progress.

Global Economic Risks

Brazil's economy is deeply intertwined with global markets, making it susceptible to external shocks. Slowdowns in key trading partners, such as the United States and China, could disrupt export flows, particularly in agriculture and hydrocarbons, which are cornerstone sectors for Brazil's trade surplus. The global demand for commodities, including soybeans, iron ore, and oil, directly affects Brazil's economic stability. For instance, a drop in oil prices could reduce revenue for Petrobras and weaken the broader fiscal outlook, while fluctuations in agricultural prices may impact rural economies and related industries.

Trade volatility is further complicated by geopolitical tensions and shifts in global supply chains. Brazil's strong reserves and flexible exchange rate system, however, act as buffers, mitigating some external risks. The government's active pursuit of trade diversification and regional integration within Mercosur and broader South-South cooperation adds further resilience to Brazil's external sector.

Major Export Partners (2023)

China: 31.9% with major imports from Brazil: Soybeans, iron ore, crude oil, and meat.

United States: 11.2% with major imports from Brazil: Aircraft, steel, coffee, and machinery.

European Union (Germany, Netherlands, etc.): 16.5% with key imports from Brazil: Coffee, beef, poultry, ethanol, and industrial products.

Argentina: 4.4%, with major imports from Brazil: Vehicles, parts, and machinery.

Japan and South Korea (Combined): ~4.8% with key imports from Brazil: Food products, iron ore, and other raw materials.

Major Export Products

- **Agricultural Products**: Soybeans (~15% of total exports), coffee, beef, poultry.
- **Minerals**: Iron ore (~12%), gold.
- **Energy**: Crude oil (~12%).
- **Manufactured Goods**: Aircraft, automobiles, machinery.

Major Import Partners (2023)

China: 22.8%, with major exports to Brazil: Electronics, machinery, chemicals, and intermediate goods.

United States: 17.7%, with major exports to Brazil: Chemicals, aerospace technology, and medical equipment.

European Union (Germany, Italy, etc.): 15.2%, with key exports to Brazil: Pharmaceuticals, automotive parts, and industrial machinery.

Argentina: 6.5%, with major exports to Brazil: Automotive parts and industrial goods.

Japan and South Korea (Combined): ~5.1% with key exports to Brazil: Electronics, heavy machinery, and vehicles.

Major Import Products

- **Industrial and Capital Goods**: Machinery, electronics, and automotive parts (~30% of imports).

- **Energy**: Refined petroleum, natural gas (~12%).
- **Chemicals**: Fertilizers, medical supplies (~10%).
- **Consumer Goods**: Electronics, clothing, and appliances.

Fiscal Discipline and Inflation Alignment

Domestically, Brazil's ability to manage fiscal and monetary policy cohesion will determine its economic trajectory. Fiscal restraint, particularly through expenditure rationalization and revenue-enhancing reforms, is crucial for aligning inflation with long-term targets. Brazil's Central Bank has demonstrated effective flexibility in managing inflation, bringing it down to 3.9% by mid-2024, and is on track to achieve the 3% target by 2026.

The government's new fiscal rule, tying expenditure growth to revenue performance, underscores its commitment to sustainability. This disciplined approach, coupled with landmark reforms like VAT simplification, positions Brazil to tackle its elevated debt-to-GDP ratio while maintaining space for essential investments in infrastructure, social services, and green initiatives.

Strategic Insights for Investors

Brazil's proactive approach to sustainable growth, digital innovation, and infrastructure development opens up diverse opportunities for investors. The following areas represent key sectors for long-term returns:

Green Infrastructure and Renewable Projects

Brazil's **Ecological Transformation Plan**, with its aggressive targets for deforestation reduction and carbon neutrality, offers significant opportunities in renewable energy, reforestation, and carbon markets. The introduction of a cap-and-trade carbon system and the voluntary carbon credit framework makes Brazil a global hub for climate finance. Investments in solar, wind, and biofuels align with both global sustainability goals and Brazil's abundant natural resources. Furthermore, the issuance of green bonds and the ECO Invest Brasil program provide platforms for international investors seeking to capitalize on Brazil's green economy.

Housing and Infrastructure Expansion

Post-disaster recovery needs, such as rebuilding after floods in Rio Grande do Sul, and ongoing urbanization trends create lucrative opportunities in Brazil's construction and infrastructure sectors. The government's focus on modernizing transportation, urban housing, and utilities aligns with the growing demand for resilient and efficient infrastructure in rapidly expanding cities like São Paulo and Rio de Janeiro. Public-private partnerships and foreign direct investment in infrastructure projects are expected to play a pivotal role in meeting these demands.

Digital and Financial Services Growth

Brazil's fintech revolution, led by **Pix** and the upcoming **Drex digital currency**, is reshaping the nation's financial ecosystem. Pix has already democratized payments, fostering financial inclusion among underserved populations, while Drex is set to tokenize the economy, enabling innovative credit mechanisms and digital asset integration. These developments create vast potential for investment in fintech startups, blockchain applications, and digital payment platforms. Brazil's regulatory environment, which supports financial innovation while ensuring security and scalability, further enhances its attractiveness as a destination for digital finance investments.

Resilience Through Strategic Innovation

By addressing global and domestic risks with targeted policies and fostering investment-friendly sectors, Brazil continues to demonstrate economic resilience. Strategic investments in green infrastructure, urban development, and digital finance will be key to unlocking Brazil's vast potential, positioning it.

Chapter Conclusion: Brazil's Renaissance: A Green and Digital Economic Powerhouse

Brazil stands at the forefront of a transformative journey, seamlessly blending its vast natural wealth with cutting-edge digital innovation to create a resilient, forward-looking economy. As the largest and most populous nation in South America, Brazil leverages its strategic geographic location, dynamic population, and abundant resources to drive sustainable growth.

The government's focus on fiscal discipline, with reforms like the VAT overhaul and new fiscal rules, ensures a stable foundation for growth while maintaining essential public investments. Inflation control, bolstered by disciplined monetary policy, has fortified Brazil's economic stability, making it an increasingly attractive destination for investors. The reduction of deforestation and the implementation of a robust carbon market underscore Brazil's leadership in global climate action, opening avenues for investments in renewable energy and ecological preservation.

On the digital frontier, Brazil's innovations such as PIX and the forthcoming Drex digital currency are revolutionizing financial inclusion and reshaping the global perception of emerging market economies. By fostering a secure and inclusive financial ecosystem, Brazil exemplifies how technology can bridge socioeconomic divides and spur growth.

In the face of global challenges, Brazil's economic adaptability, commitment to sustainability, and digital transformation reinforce its position as a global leader in both innovation and ecological stewardship. The nation's proactive policies and thriving sectors—from green energy to fintech—offer unparalleled opportunities for investors, cementing Brazil's role as a beacon of resilience and progress in the 21st century.

Chapter (3)

Russia: A Pivotal Global Player Navigating Economic and Investment Challenges

"BRICS is one of the key elements of the emerging multipolar world order, which increasingly reflects the interests and aspirations of the states of both the global South and the East.

Vladimir Putin, President of Russia:

Step into the vast landscape that is Russia—a country rich in natural resources and strategic influence, yet navigating a complex tapestry of economic, investment, and regulatory reforms amidst international scrutiny. Against a backdrop of sanctions, geopolitical tensions, and a drive for economic diversification, Russia's resilience shines through its abundant resources and strategic initiatives. As the largest country in the world, Russia offers unique opportunities for investors willing to navigate a challenging yet dynamic landscape.

Spanning two continents and 11 time zones, Russia is the largest country in the world, covering over 17 million square kilometers. Its unique geographical position connects Europe and Asia, offering immense strategic advantages. With a population of over 140 million, concentrated primarily in the western regions, Russia's demographic profile is aging but educated, boasting a literacy rate of 99.7%. The country's nominal GDP was $2.021 trillion in 2023, while its purchasing power parity (PPP) GDP reached an impressive $5.816 trillion, ranking fourth globally. These figures underscore Russia's significance as an economic powerhouse, albeit one navigating the complexities of global geopolitics and domestic challenges.

Economic Resilience in the Face of Adversity

Russia's economy is marked by stark contrasts: immense resource wealth and industrial capability on one hand, and challenges stemming from sanctions, corruption, and limited green infrastructure on the other. Despite these obstacles, the country's economic performance remains robust:

GDP Growth Trajectory: After a contraction of 2.07% in 2022 due to geopolitical tensions and sanctions, Russia rebounded with a 3.6% GDP growth rate in 2023. This recovery reflects the economy's adaptability, underpinned by strategic exports, domestic consumption, and state-led initiatives.

Unemployment Rate: At 3.33% in 2023, unemployment in Russia is remarkably low, showcasing a resilient labor market. Youth unemployment, however, stands higher at 12.7%, highlighting opportunities for targeted employment strategies in emerging industries.

Public Debt: Russia maintains one of the world's lowest public debt-to-GDP ratios, at just 19.51% in 2022. This fiscal prudence provides a buffer against economic shocks and reflects the government's cautious borrowing practices. Private debt levels, while less transparent, are supported by a stable banking sector.

Income Inequality: With a Gini index of 36 (2020), Russia faces moderate income inequality, though disparities persist between urban and rural areas. Efforts to diversify the economy and foster inclusive growth remain essential to addressing this gap.

Sectoral Contributions to GDP: Services account for 56.9% of GDP, while industry contributes 30.6%, and agriculture a modest 3.3%. This structure highlights the dominance of urbanized and industrialized sectors, with potential for growth in technology, agriculture, and renewable energy.

A Global Player in Trade and Energy

Russia's trade relationships and energy exports remain pillars of its economic profile, reinforcing its position as a critical player in the global market:

Export Dynamics

Energy commodities dominate Russia's export portfolio, reflecting its role as one of the world's leading energy exporters. In 2023, crude petroleum, natural gas, and refined petroleum collectively constituted a substantial portion of its $465.4 billion export revenue. Fertilizers and coal are also significant export products, underscoring the diversity of its energy-related commodities. Key trading partners include:

- **China**: Receiving 21% of exports in 2022, China remains Russia's largest trading partner, benefiting from energy supplies and other goods.

- **India**: Accounting for 8% of exports, India's increasing energy demands have made it a growing market for Russian oil and gas.
- **Germany**: As Europe's largest economy, Germany received 6% of Russia's exports in 2022, primarily energy resources.
- **Italy and Turkey**: Each accounted for 5% of exports, highlighting their importance as strategic European and regional partners for energy trade.

This export landscape showcases Russia's ability to diversify markets and maintain significant trade flows despite geopolitical pressures.

Foreign Exchange Reserves

Russia's robust foreign exchange and gold reserves, valued at $597.2 billion in 2023, provide a substantial buffer against economic shocks and sanctions. Ranked fourth globally in reserve holdings, these assets enable the country to stabilize its currency, fund critical imports, and maintain investor confidence. Gold reserves, in particular, play a critical role in mitigating risks associated with volatile global financial markets.

Inflation Control and Monetary Policy

Inflation management has been a cornerstone of Russia's economic resilience. After peaking in earlier years, inflation rates stabilized at 6.69% in 2021, with further improvement observed through subsequent targeted monetary policies. The

Central Bank of Russia has employed interest rate adjustments and currency interventions to curb inflationary pressures, ensuring greater economic stability amid fluctuating global conditions.

Geopolitical Realignment in Trade

Russia has strategically realigned its trade relationships in response to sanctions and shifting global dynamics. While historically reliant on European markets, recent years have seen a decisive pivot toward Asian and Middle Eastern partners. This strategy ensures sustained demand for its energy exports and creates opportunities for expanding trade in non-energy sectors, such as agriculture and industrial machinery.

Energy Infrastructure and Technological Advancements

Investments in advanced energy infrastructure, including pipelines, liquefied natural gas (LNG) terminals, and Arctic exploration, have enhanced Russia's ability to deliver energy efficiently to global markets. Its polar-class icebreakers facilitate year-round access to the Arctic, where untapped reserves promise long-term energy security. Furthermore, technological advancements in extraction and refining bolster the competitiveness of its energy products.

Broader Trade Profile

While energy dominates, Russia's trade portfolio also includes agricultural products such as wheat and sunflower oil, reflecting its leadership in global food markets. Other significant exports include fertilizers, industrial metals, and machinery, highlighting a broader economic base capable of supporting diverse trade relationships.

By leveraging its abundant natural resources, managing inflation effectively, and recalibrating its trade strategies, Russia remains a formidable player in the global trade and energy sectors. Its ability to adapt to shifting geopolitical landscapes ensures continued economic influence on the world stage.

U.S. Sanctions on Russia: Impact and Effectiveness

The U.S., alongside allies, has implemented unprecedented sanctions against Russia in response to its invasion of Ukraine. These measures have targeted Russia's financial, military, and energy sectors, with the goal of crippling its ability to sustain aggression. The sanctions' effectiveness and Russia's reactions provide insights into the challenges and successes of economic statecraft.

Sanctions Implemented

Financial Isolation:

- Major Russian banks sanctioned, many removed from the SWIFT financial system.
- Central Bank reserves immobilized, cutting off access to $300 billion in foreign assets.

Export Controls:

- Restrictions on dual-use technologies, semiconductors, and high-tech goods critical for defense and industrial sectors.
- Sanctions on key defense entities like Rostec and United Aircraft Corporation.

Energy Measures:

Exploration of G7-led price caps on Russian oil and bans on certain exports.

Targeting Oligarchs and Elites:

Over 1,000 individuals and entities sanctioned, freezing billions in assets globally. For example, on 28th April 2022, the US sanctioned one of Russia's largest state-owned enterprises, the joint stock company United Shipbuilding Corporation, that builds Russia's largest warships. Additionally the sanction extended to include 28 of its subsidiaries and eight members of its board of directors.

Furthermore, two vital companies to the Russian defence like Rostec, United Aircraft Corporation, and United Engine Corporation were all sanctioned on 28 June 2022. Rostec is regarded as Russia's most important defense conglomerate. The United Aircraft Corporation builds and maintains Russia's combat aircraft. And the United Engine Corporation develops, produces engines for Russia's – for Russian weapon systems, including aircraft and naval vessels.

Quantified Economic Impact on Russia

Economic Metrics

GDP Decline: during the Foreign Press Center (FPC) briefing about U.S. sanctions against Russia held in Washington on 13 July 2022 with representatives from the Bureau of European and Eurasian Affairs, the representatives projected contraction of the Russian economy to be anything between 11.2% (world bank projection) and 16% in 2022 and near future, marking the steepest economic decline in Russia in nearly 30 years. What happened in reality was that Russia's GDP contracted by only 2.07% in 2022, less severe than some forecasts but indicative of economic strain.

Inflation: Peaked at nearly 16%, eroding consumer purchasing power.

Oil and Gas Revenues: In 2023, Russia's oil and gas tax revenues fell by 24% to 8.8 trillion rubles ($99.4 billion) compared to 2022, mainly due to lower oil prices.

Industrial Output: Car production in Russia fell by 67% in 2022, reflecting disruptions in manufacturing due to sanctions.

Exports Collapse: U.S. exports to Russia decreased by 96%, while global semiconductor shipments to Russia fell by 90%, crippling manufacturing and technology sectors.

Corporate Exodus: Over 700 international companies exited Russia, causing supply chain disruptions and reducing foreign investment.

Energy Sector: Despite higher global energy prices, sanctions reduced Russian oil exports to the EU by two-thirds. The G7 price cap on oil aims to further restrict revenue while maintaining global supply stability.

Russia's Reactions and Adaptations

Capital Controls: Measures like currency restrictions temporarily stabilized the ruble but exposed vulnerabilities to external shocks.

Trade Diversion: Russia increased exports to non-sanctioning countries like China and India, though at reduced efficiency and profitability.

Domestic Adjustments: Attempted self-reliance in technology and manufacturing, often with subpar substitutes.

Effectiveness of Sanctions

Short-Term Effects:

- Severe economic shock immediately disrupted financial systems, trade, and supply chains.
- Russia's defense industry was directly impacted, with production delays and equipment shortages.

Long-Term Weakening:

- Technology restrictions have impaired Russia's ability to sustain advanced military production.
- Economic isolation will continue to erode Russia's growth potential and global influence.

Global Stability and Deterrence:

- Demonstrated unity among democracies in defending international norms and opposing aggression.
- Set a precedent for coordinated global responses to future crises.

Challenges and Gaps

Energy Revenues: Initially, higher global energy prices mitigated some losses from reduced exports. The effectiveness of price caps is key to addressing this gap.

Evasion Attempts: Russia's trade adjustments and use of alternative financial systems reduced some sanctions' effectiveness, emphasizing the need for enforcement mechanisms.

Overall assessment of sanctions on Russia

The U.S. sanctions have significantly weakened Russia's economy, reduced its ability to fund and sustain military aggression, and isolated it from global financial systems. The sanctions' full effectiveness will become more apparent over time as cumulative economic damage and enforcement efforts compound.

While Russia has shown resilience in certain areas, the projected economic contraction and technological degradation highlight the sanctions' success in imposing long-term costs. These measures reaffirm global commitment to Ukraine's sovereignty and deter similar aggressions in the future.

Strategic Resilience Amid Sanctions

The Russian economy's ability to withstand international sanctions exemplifies a remarkable strategic resilience, underscored by adaptations in key sectors and a focus on self-reliance:

Sanctions-Induced Adaptation

The imposition of sanctions has catalyzed Russia's pivot toward self-sufficiency in critical sectors, significantly reducing reliance on foreign imports. Agriculture has flourished, with Russia becoming a global leader in wheat production. Domestic pharmaceutical and defense manufacturing capacities have expanded, addressing vulnerabilities in supply chains and fostering innovation. The focus on local production has been instrumental in shielding the economy from external shocks.

Energy Independence and Diversification

Energy continues to play a central role in Russia's economic resilience. Approximately 40% of its electricity generation is sourced from nuclear and hydroelectric power, reducing dependency on fossil fuels and showcasing investments in sustainable energy infrastructure. The nation's substantial reserves of natural gas and oil bolster its position as a leading energy exporter, even under constrained global conditions. Moreover, Russia's commitment to developing renewable energy sources, such as wind and solar, although modest, signals a recognition of future energy diversification.

Industrial and Technological Strength

Russia maintains a comprehensive industrial base capable of producing advanced military, aerospace, and transport technologies. Its defense industry not only satisfies domestic needs but also contributes significantly to exports, making Russia the world's second-largest military hardware supplier. Advances in machine building, electronics, and high-tech equipment manufacturing highlight the nation's capacity to innovate under pressure.

Economic and Trade Adaptations

Despite sanctions, Russia's trade partnerships have undergone significant realignment. China has emerged as the primary trading partner, accounting for over 20% of exports. New agreements with India, Turkey, and other nations emphasize strategic pivots toward non-Western markets. These shifts ensure a steady inflow of revenues and strengthen geopolitical alliances.

Sustainable Resource Utilization

Rich in natural resources, Russia has leveraged its vast reserves of oil, gas, and strategic minerals to maintain economic stability. Investments in mining and extraction technologies have optimized resource utilization, while forestry and agricultural land use have been carefully managed to support long-term sustainability.

Infrastructure and Connectivity Enhancements

Extensive infrastructure projects, including railway expansions and port upgrades, support domestic economic integration and facilitate trade. Russia's vast network of waterways and polar-class icebreakers ensures access to Arctic resources and shipping lanes, enhancing its strategic connectivity in global trade.

By emphasizing self-reliance, diversifying energy sources, and realigning trade partnerships, Russia demonstrates an adaptive economic strategy capable of weathering external pressures while fostering long-term growth and resilience.

Demographics and Workforce: Challenges and Opportunities

The demographic profile of Russia presents both hurdles and prospects:

Population Growth Decline: Russia's population growth rate stands at -0.49% (2024), driven by low birth rates (8.4 births per 1,000 people) and a high median age of 41.9 years. This demographic trend poses long-term challenges for workforce sustainability.

Educated Workforce: With 16 years of school life expectancy and near-universal literacy, Russia boasts a highly skilled labor force, essential for sectors such as technology, healthcare, and advanced manufacturing.

Russia's economic landscape combines resilience with room for improvement. While fiscal stability and resource wealth provide a strong foundation, long-term growth hinges on diversifying its economy, addressing demographic challenges, and fostering innovation.

Regulatory Reforms and Investment Potential

Russia's regulatory landscape is evolving, addressing longstanding challenges to attract foreign and domestic investments:

Taxation Reforms: Recent measures have focused on refining tax systems to enhance compliance and competitiveness. Tax revenue as a percentage of GDP is at 10.97%, indicating room for growth through progressive measures like closing loopholes and fostering transparency.

Green Transition Efforts: Although fossil fuels dominate energy production, efforts are underway to expand renewable energy sources. With 19.2% of electricity generated from hydroelectricity and 19.6% from nuclear energy, Russia shows a steady transition toward sustainable practices.

Encouraging Innovation: The sanctions have spurred innovation in key sectors like telecommunications and pharmaceuticals. Russia's investments in 5G deployment, AI, and biotechnology indicate a forward-looking approach to securing economic sovereignty.

These reforms aim to enhance investor confidence while addressing systemic inefficiencies and modernizing economic frameworks.

Key Investment Sectors: Opportunities Amidst Challenges

Amid its challenges, Russia offers lucrative investment opportunities across a variety of high-growth sectors:

Energy and Commodities: Beyond oil and natural gas, Russia is expanding its nuclear and hydroelectric capacities. Its coal production of over 508 million metric tons (2022) highlights opportunities for energy diversification.

Technology and Telecommunications: Russia's focus on developing fiber-optic infrastructure and AI positions it as a potential tech hub. However, the military's restrictions on 5G spectrum remain a challenge.

Agriculture and Food Security: As one of the largest wheat exporters globally, Russia leverages its vast arable land. Agricultural products like sugar beets, sunflowers, and barley showcase its strength in agribusiness.

Infrastructure Development: With over 85,000 km of railways and 1.28 million km of roadways, infrastructure development remains a priority. Initiatives to modernize its ports and icebreaker fleet signal opportunities in logistics.

These sectors align with Russia's domestic priorities and international aspirations, offering diverse opportunities for investment.

Balancing Risks and Rewards

Navigating the Russian investment landscape demands a nuanced approach. Key factors to consider include:

Geopolitical Risks: The conflict in Ukraine and international sanctions create uncertainties that require careful risk management.

Emerging Market Dynamics: Russia's strategic partnerships within the Eurasian Economic Union and with nations like China and India highlight opportunities in non-Western trade dynamics.

Sustainability and Innovation: Investments in ESG-aligned projects, like renewable energy or sustainable infrastructure, can mitigate risks and align with global trends.

Understanding these dynamics is critical for investors aiming to capitalize on Russia's potential while managing exposure to its challenges.

Chapter Conclusion: The Future Beckons: Opportunities for Visionary Investors

Russia's economic and investment trajectory is defined by its resource wealth, strategic reforms, and an evolving global role. For investors willing to engage strategically, Russia offers a rich tapestry of opportunities in energy, technology, agriculture, and infrastructure. Despite challenges, the country's focus on innovation and sustainability provides a compelling case for long-term investment.

Are you ready to explore the vast opportunities in Russia's evolving economy? With strategic planning and informed choices, the rewards of investing in this resilient global player could be profound.

Chapter (4)

India's Economic Outlook: Resilience Amid Challenges and Strategic Reforms for Sustainable Growth

"As a diverse and inclusive platform, BRICS can play a positive role in all areas."

Narendra Modi, Prime Minister of India

India is firmly positioned as one of the world's most dynamic and rapidly growing economies. Located in Southern Asia, the country occupies a pivotal geographical position bordered by the Arabian Sea and the Bay of Bengal, nestled between Burma and Pakistan. With a total area of approximately 3.29 million square kilometers, India ranks as the seventh-largest country in the world by land area, slightly over one-third the size of the United States. Its land boundaries stretch across 13,888 kilometers, bordering six countries, including China, Nepal, and Bangladesh. The nation also boasts a coastline of 7,000 kilometers, emphasizing its strategic access to vital Indian Ocean trade routes.

India is the second-most populous country globally, with an estimated population of over 1.4 billion in 2024. This vast population is not only diverse, with over 22 officially recognized languages, but also youthful, with a median age of 29.8 years. This demographic dividend, coupled with a labor force participation rate of nearly 68%, positions India as a reservoir of talent and economic potential. However, challenges such as disparities in regional development, urban-rural divides, and environmental pressures remain prominent.

The nation's climate varies significantly, ranging from tropical monsoons in the south to temperate conditions in the north, which has shaped its diverse terrain, including the Himalayas, the fertile plains of the Ganges, and the arid regions of the Thar Desert. Its rich natural resource base includes coal (ranking fourth in reserves globally), iron ore, natural gas, and agricultural land, underpinning its industrial and agrarian sectors.

With a long history rooted in the Indus Valley civilization and subsequent empires, India has evolved into a federal parliamentary republic. The capital, New Delhi, serves as the political and administrative hub, while cities like Mumbai, Bangalore, and Kolkata drive economic and technological growth. This historical depth combined with robust public investment, expanding services, and global integration continues to propel India's economic narrative, making it a key player on the global stage.

India's Robust Growth Story: Powered by Consumption and Public Investment

India's economy is projected to grow at 6.3% in both FY2023/24 and FY2024/25, reflecting its resilience and adaptability amidst a challenging global economic environment. In FY2022/23, real GDP growth reached 7.2%, a moderation from the remarkable 9.1% seen in FY2021/22 but still indicative of a strong recovery from the COVID-19 pandemic.

India's GDP in nominal terms is on track to cross the **$5 trillion mark by FY2026/27**, while its PPP-adjusted GDP will likely exceed **$15 trillion by the end of the decade**, reinforcing its role as a global economic powerhouse. India's GDP growth is expected to stabilize around **6-6.5% annually** over the next five years, supported by strong domestic demand, public investment, and productivity gains from digital infrastructure. The PPP-adjusted GDP trajectory highlights India's position as the **third-largest economy globally by purchasing power**, after China and the United States.

This sustained growth is fueled by robust domestic demand, a thriving services sector, and the government's strategic emphasis on infrastructure development. According to the IMF, these growth drivers include pent-up household demand, significant public sector capital expenditure, and a surge in outsourcing-related services exports as global economies recover.

India's public investment strategy has become a cornerstone of its economic policy. The government has implemented ambitious capital expenditure plans to address critical infrastructure deficits, particularly in energy, transportation, and urban development. In FY2023/24, public capital expenditure is expected to reach unprecedented levels, aiming to stimulate private sector investment by improving connectivity, reducing logistics costs, and enhancing overall business efficiency. Public-private partnerships (PPPs) have gained momentum, fostering collaboration between the public and private sectors and unlocking additional investment potential.

Infrastructure investment remains a powerful driver of economic activity. For instance, India's urban infrastructure requirements are projected to need over 1.2% of GDP annually through 2036 to address the demands of rapid urbanization. The government's initiatives, such as the National Infrastructure Pipeline and PM Gati Shakti—an integrated approach to logistics and supply chain management—are strategically designed to bridge infrastructure gaps and fuel long-term growth.

The services sector, a cornerstone of India's economy, continues to thrive, driven by robust growth in IT and business process outsourcing (BPO) services. India's digital infrastructure has been instrumental in boosting productivity and enhancing financial inclusion. Key innovations like the Unified Payments Interface (UPI) and Aadhaar-based identification have revolutionized access to financial services, accelerating consumption and investment across demographic segments.

Although the consumption surge from post-pandemic pent-up demand has begun to moderate, it is being replaced by an encouraging rise in private sector investment. The recovery in private investment is supported by easing financial conditions, government incentives, and improvements in corporate balance sheets. Resilient consumer demand, especially in urban areas, and an expanding middle class further bolster this trend.

The government's focus on digital transformation has also become a crucial enabler of economic growth. Investments in digital public infrastructure, such as the India Stack, have created opportunities for startups, innovation, and efficiency gains in both public services and private enterprises. By fostering a vibrant digital ecosystem, India is poised to enhance productivity across sectors, opening avenues for sustained long-term growth.

India's resilience in the face of global economic headwinds underscores its structural strengths and policy agility. With a balanced mix of consumption, investment, and innovation, the country is not only a significant driver of regional economic momentum but also a compelling destination for global investment.

Inflation: Managing Volatility Amid Structural Shocks

Inflation remains a key challenge for India, reflecting both structural and cyclical factors. In July 2023, headline inflation peaked at 7.4%, driven largely by a sharp surge in food prices, particularly vegetables. This spike was fueled by weather-related supply shocks, including a staggering 202% year-on-year increase in tomato prices, exacerbated by uneven monsoons and disruptions in agricultural supply chains. Such price volatility highlights the vulnerability of India's inflation dynamics to exogenous shocks, particularly in the food sector.

Despite these pressures, inflationary trends began to moderate by August 2023 as food prices stabilized, and by September, the Consumer Price Index (CPI) inflation returned to within the Reserve Bank of India's (RBI) target band of 4±2%. The IMF projects inflation to further ease to an average of 5.4% in FY2023/24, supported by effective monetary policy measures and the anticipated stabilization of global commodity prices. Over the medium term, headline inflation is expected to converge toward the RBI's 4% target, contingent on continued fiscal and monetary prudence.

Core Inflation and Policy Response

Core inflation, which excludes volatile food and fuel prices, has also shown signs of moderation, falling to 4.5%

by September 2023. This reflects the RBI's proactive monetary tightening, which successfully anchored inflation expectations and dampened second-round effects from previous price shocks. The central bank's data-dependent approach, including a neutral monetary stance, has allowed it to respond effectively to inflationary pressures without stifling economic growth. The RBI's policies are complemented by government interventions, such as export restrictions on essential commodities like rice and wheat, which were aimed at stabilizing domestic food prices.

Structural Drivers of Inflation

India's inflation dynamics are distinct due to the significant weight of food prices in the CPI basket—nearly 50%, compared to much lower shares in other emerging markets. This makes the CPI highly sensitive to agricultural shocks, which are often driven by erratic weather patterns, such as monsoons, droughts, or floods. Such shocks can cause persistent inflation volatility, particularly in a country where a large portion of household consumption is directed toward food and essential goods.

The structural nature of food inflation is further amplified by supply chain inefficiencies, including inadequate storage facilities, post-harvest losses, and logistics challenges. The government has been investing in agricultural infrastructure and logistics to address these inefficiencies, but significant gaps remain.

Risks and Outlook

Food price volatility, driven by climate-related risks and global supply chain disruptions, continues to pose a significant threat to India's inflation trajectory. Additionally, India's heavy reliance on imported energy leaves it exposed to fluctuations in global oil and gas prices, which can have cascading effects on transportation and overall production costs. Domestically, fiscal pressures to manage cost-of-living increases through subsidies or price controls could further complicate inflation management.

The RBI has maintained a vigilant stance, ready to adjust monetary policy as needed to counter inflationary risks. However, the central bank faces a delicate balancing act: containing inflation without curbing economic momentum, especially as private investment begins to recover.

Policy Priorities for Inflation Management

To mitigate inflation volatility, both immediate and structural measures are necessary. The RBI's focus on price stability, coupled with the government's fiscal policies aimed at improving agricultural productivity and supply chain resilience, will be critical. Additionally, investment in climate-resilient agriculture, combined with initiatives to strengthen food storage and distribution networks, can help reduce the frequency and severity of food price shocks.

Over the medium term, achieving the RBI's 4% inflation target sustainably will require core inflation to remain anchored around 4% while allowing for temporary volatility in food prices. Temporary government interventions, such as export restrictions or subsidies, may be justified during major supply shocks but must be phased out promptly to restore market equilibrium.

India's inflation management reflects the complexities of balancing structural vulnerabilities with the need for macroeconomic stability. While recent trends indicate progress, the path to stable and sustainable inflation is fraught with risks from exogenous shocks, particularly in food and energy prices. As the government and the RBI work in tandem to address these challenges, India's ability to maintain inflation within target ranges will play a pivotal role in sustaining its economic growth and fostering long-term investment confidence.

Fiscal Policy: Debt Sustainability and Medium-Term Challenges

India's fiscal landscape continues to face significant challenges, with the fiscal deficit remaining elevated despite efforts at consolidation. In FY2022/23, the central government's fiscal deficit stood at 6.5% of GDP, improving from pandemic-induced highs but still reflecting substantial fiscal strain. Projections indicate a modest reduction to 6.0% in FY2023/24, supported by strong revenue performance and restrained expenditure growth. However, India's public debt remains high, with the debt-to-GDP ratio projected to reach 82% in FY2023/24, necessitating decisive fiscal reforms to ensure long-term sustainability.

Fiscal Strategy: Balancing Growth and Consolidation

India's fiscal policy aims to strike a delicate balance between supporting economic growth through capital investment and pursuing medium-term fiscal consolidation. Public investment in infrastructure, a central plank of fiscal policy, has been critical in sustaining growth momentum, with the government's capital expenditure reaching a record 3.3% of GDP in FY2023/24. However, maintaining this growth-supportive spending while managing rising debt levels is a complex challenge.

Revenue Mobilization: Leveraging Digitalization and Tax Reform

Enhancing revenue mobilization is key to improving fiscal sustainability. India has made significant progress in strengthening its tax administration, particularly through the implementation of the **Goods and Services Tax (GST)** and the adoption of digital technologies. The GST, which unifies indirect taxes across the country, has improved tax compliance and widened the tax base.

Monthly GST collections consistently exceed ₹1.5 trillion ($18 billion), reflecting the system's growing efficiency.

Despite these gains, India's tax-to-GDP ratio remains lower than that of many peer economies, underscoring the need for further reforms. Expanding the tax base is paramount, particularly through measures to improve direct tax compliance, rationalize tax exemptions, and introduce progressive taxation. Enhancing digital systems, such as e-invoicing and AI-driven audits, can further streamline tax collection, reduce evasion, and boost revenues.

Spending Efficiency: Targeting Subsidies and Strengthening Social Support

On the expenditure side, improving the efficiency of public spending is critical. Subsidies, particularly in food, fuel, and fertilizers, continue to place a significant burden on India's fiscal resources. Rationalizing these subsidies by targeting them more effectively to vulnerable populations is vital.

India's use of **digital identification systems** like Aadhaar has already transformed social welfare delivery, enabling the government to implement **Direct Benefit Transfers (DBTs)** that minimize leakage and improve subsidy targeting. For example, fuel and cooking gas subsidies are now directly credited to beneficiaries' bank accounts, reducing fiscal costs and ensuring that assistance reaches those in need.

In addition to subsidy rationalization, prioritizing capital expenditure over current expenditure is vital. Investments in infrastructure, healthcare, and education yield higher long-term economic returns compared to untargeted spending.

Public Debt Sustainability: Risks and Mitigation

India's public debt composition mitigates some risks, as the majority of its debt is denominated in domestic currency and held by residents. This reduces vulnerabilities to exchange rate fluctuations and external shocks. Additionally, India benefits from a favorable interest-growth differential, which helps manage debt servicing costs despite elevated debt levels.

However, fiscal buffers remain insufficient to address future shocks. External risks, including global economic fragmentation and commodity price volatility, could exacerbate fiscal pressures. Domestically, weather-related shocks and election-related spending in 2024 could further strain public finances. A **fiscal consolidation path** that combines enhanced revenue mobilization with expenditure rationalization is therefore recommended. This includes better prioritization of government spending, increased transparency in public accounts, and a gradual reduction in the fiscal deficit to reach the central government's target of **4.5% of GDP by FY2025/26**.

Long-Term Fiscal Reforms

In the medium to long term, India must address structural issues to achieve sustainable fiscal management. Key priorities include:

Deepening GST Reforms: Simplifying tax slabs and rationalizing exemptions can enhance revenue efficiency.

Enhancing Health and Education Spending: Allocating greater resources to human capital development is crucial for inclusive growth.

Investing in Climate Resilience: With increasing risks from climate change, targeted investments in climate-resilient infrastructure and sustainable energy are essential.

India's fiscal policy reflects the complexities of balancing growth and consolidation in a rapidly evolving economic landscape. While public investment continues to drive economic momentum, high debt levels and fiscal deficits necessitate urgent reforms. Through enhanced revenue mobilization, targeted subsidies, and improved spending efficiency, India can strengthen its fiscal framework and build resilience against future shocks. Achieving fiscal sustainability will not only stabilize public finances but also reinforce India's position as one of the world's most dynamic economies.

Debt Dynamics: Sovereign Risks and the Need for Fiscal Reforms

India's debt profile highlights both strengths and vulnerabilities. The country's public debt is predominantly composed of **long-term, fixed-rate instruments denominated in local currency**, mitigating risks from exchange rate fluctuations and global interest rate volatility. However, the sheer volume of debt poses a formidable challenge. Public debt as a percentage of GDP is expected to peak at **82% in FY2024/25**, before gradually declining over the medium term, provided fiscal consolidation efforts stay on track. G**ross financing needs remain substantial**, averaging around 15% of GDP in the medium term per IMF, which emphasizes the importance of a prudent debt management strategy.

India's relatively **low external debt**, approximately 18% of GDP as of FY2022/23, provides some insulation from external financial shocks. The bulk of this debt is long-term and concessional, reflecting India's proactive external borrowing policies. Nevertheless, vulnerabilities persist, especially from **contingent liabilities**. One key area of concern is the electricity distribution sector, which has historically required frequent state intervention. Structural reforms are needed to address inefficiencies in this sector, including reducing transmission losses, improving billing and collection efficiency, and introducing cost-reflective tariffs. Without such reforms, contingent liabilities could escalate, adding to fiscal pressures.

India's favorable **interest-growth differential**—where economic growth outpaces interest rates on public debt—offers an opportunity to gradually reduce debt without resorting to severe expenditure cuts. However, this requires consistent adherence to fiscal discipline and measures to ensure that public investments generate high economic returns.

Debt Sustainability Outlook

Global economic uncertainties, rising energy prices, or adverse weather events could disrupt the trajectory of fiscal consolidation. Additionally, external shocks could amplify financing pressures, given India's reliance on domestic savings for funding its high fiscal deficits. The government's commitment to a **4.5% fiscal deficit target by FY2025/26** will be critical for ensuring debt sustainability, alongside continued efforts to crowd in private investment through public infrastructure spending.

External Sector: Strengthening Resilience Amid Global Volatility

India's external sector has demonstrated resilience despite global financial volatility. By mid-2023, foreign exchange reserves had recovered to **$587 billion**, covering more than seven months of imports. These reserves provide a vital buffer against external shocks, including commodity price spikes and geopolitical tensions. India's position as a major player in global services exports, particularly in IT and business process outsourcing, has further strengthened its external sector.

Current Account Dynamics

The current account deficit (CAD) widened to **2% of GDP in FY2022/23**, driven by higher commodity imports and a post-pandemic surge in domestic demand. However, the IMF projects the CAD to narrow to **1.8% of GDP in FY2023/24**, supported by robust services exports and reduced oil import costs. India's increasing energy diversification, including a **40% share of discounted Russian oil in its imports by mid-2023**, has been pivotal in lowering import bills. These measures, coupled with resilient remittance inflows, contribute to improving the external account balance.

Trade and Geopolitical Challenges

Despite these positive developments, external risks remain significant. The **global growth slowdown** poses a threat to India's export-driven sectors, particularly IT and manufacturing. Geopolitical tensions and commodity price volatility could further strain India's trade balance, especially given its reliance on imported energy and raw materials. Supply chain disruptions, exacerbated by conflicts or natural disasters, also pose risks to export competitiveness and import stability. India's trade is characterized by:

- A strong focus on petroleum products, textiles, and software exports.
- High dependence on energy imports, particularly from the Middle East.
- Trade relations with key global economies such as the **U.S.**, **China**, and **UAE**, with growing ties in Asia and Europe.

This following list highlights the diversity of India's trade relations and product categories.

Main Export Partners

United States: 18.1%, **United Arab Emirates (UAE)**: 7.1%, **China**: 5.1%, **Bangladesh**: 4.3%, and **Netherlands**: 3.7%. Key Export Products:

- **Petroleum products**: Refined fuels form a significant share of India's exports.
- **Gems and jewelry**: Diamonds and gold jewelry are among the leading exports.
- **Pharmaceuticals**: India is a major global supplier of generic medicines.
- **Machinery and equipment**: Electrical machinery and industrial equipment are prominent.

- **Textiles and garments**: India is a leading exporter of cotton, fabrics, and finished garments.
- **Agricultural products**: Includes rice, tea, spices, and sugar.
- **Software and IT services**: Export of IT and business process outsourcing services.

Main Import Partners (2021)

China: 16.5%, **United Arab Emirates (UAE)**: 6.7%, **United States**: 6.2%, **Saudi Arabia**: 5.6% and **Iraq**: 5.0%. Key Import Products:

- **Crude petroleum and related products**: India heavily relies on imports for its energy needs.
- **Gold and silver**: Precious metals account for a significant share of imports.
- **Electronics**: Mobile phones, semiconductors, and other electronics form a major import category.
- **Machinery and equipment**: Industrial machinery, electrical equipment, and components.
- **Chemicals and fertilizers**: Used extensively in agriculture and industry.
- **Coal and natural gas**: Energy imports also include coal and LNG to meet industrial and power sector demands.

- **Edible oils**: Includes palm oil and soybean oil to meet domestic food requirements.

Policy Priorities for External Resilience

Strengthening external sector resilience can be achieved though:

Export diversification: Reducing dependence on specific markets or sectors, particularly through increased focus on manufacturing exports and emerging markets.

Energy security: Continuing efforts to diversify energy sources, including investments in renewables and partnerships for critical minerals.

Exchange rate flexibility: Allowing the rupee to adjust to market dynamics while limiting foreign exchange interventions to disorderly market conditions.

India's **trade policy** also plays a critical role. While recent export restrictions on food items such as rice and wheat have addressed domestic supply concerns, removing these restrictions in the medium term may help to avoid distorting global trade and incentivizing domestic production.

Outlook for the External Sector

India's external position is expected to remain stable, supported by its strong services sector, resilient remittance flows, and growing energy independence. However, **structural reforms in trade and manufacturing** are necessary to further strengthen the balance of payments and reduce vulnerabilities to global shocks. Continuous emphasis on infrastructure and digital public goods will enable India to remain a global leader in services exports, while domestic manufacturing reforms under initiatives like **Make in India** and **PLI (Production Linked Incentive) schemes** can help boost competitiveness.

India's external sector resilience hinges on its ability to navigate global volatility while leveraging structural strengths in services and energy. The government's focus on economic diversification, combined with prudent fiscal and monetary policies, will be pivotal in safeguarding external stability and sustaining economic growth.

Financial Sector Resilience: Managing Risk in a Growing Market

India's financial sector has showcased notable resilience, supported by improved capital buffers, reduced non-performing assets (NPAs), and strengthened profitability in the banking system. As of March 2023, the capital-to-risk-weighted assets ratio (CRAR) reached a record **17.2%**, underlining the sector's robust capitalization. Bank profitability has also surged, with return on assets and net interest margins improving significantly, reflecting prudent risk management and a favorable interest rate environment. Meanwhile, NPA ratios declined to **multi-year lows of 5%**, contributing to enhanced systemic stability.

The financial sector's strength is bolstered by comprehensive regulatory oversight from the **Reserve Bank of India (RBI)**, which has consistently implemented measures to address vulnerabilities. Efforts to improve credit underwriting standards, enhance loan recovery mechanisms, and tighten provisioning norms have collectively contributed to reducing systemic risk.

Challenges in Non-Bank Financial Companies (NBFCs) and Urban Cooperative Banks (UCBs)

Despite these achievements, the financial sector continues to face challenges. Smaller non-bank financial companies (NBFCs) and urban cooperative banks (UCBs) remain vulnerable to **liquidity and credit risks**. Many NBFCs, which play a critical role in financing underserved segments, face challenges in accessing stable funding sources, making them susceptible to market volatility. Similarly, urban cooperative banks, which serve localized markets, often lack the robust risk management frameworks seen in larger banks, leaving them exposed to governance and credit quality issues.

The rapid growth in **personal loans**, which recorded a **16.1% year-on-year increase** by March 2023, has raised concerns about potential financial stress. Unsecured loans, particularly in the retail segment, require careful monitoring, as their rapid expansion could amplify risks in the event of economic downturns.

Policy Recommendations and Supervisory Vigilance

Sustained vigilance in banking sector supervision is vital. The RBI will need to continue employing prudential tools to mitigate emerging risks, particularly in segments showing rapid credit expansion. Enhanced stress testing, risk-based supervision, and strengthened governance in public sector banks (PSBs) will be critical to maintaining financial stability.

Expanding **access to credit for small and medium enterprises (SMEs)** is another crucial area. SMEs, which are vital to India's economic fabric, often face financing constraints due to perceived credit risks. Encouraging financial innovation, such as **fintech-driven solutions**, and deepening capital markets can improve credit flow to these businesses.

Structural Reforms: Key to Unlocking India's Potential for Inclusive Growth

India's vast demographic advantage—anchored by its young and growing population—offers unparalleled opportunities for economic growth. However, fully unlocking this potential requires **comprehensive structural reforms** that address systemic inefficiencies and foster inclusive development.

Labor Market Reforms and Female Workforce Participation

India's labor market remains characterized by a large informal sector and relatively low female labor force participation (FLFP), which stands at approximately 24.5%. Modernizing labor laws, simplifying regulations, and creating a more flexible labor environment to encourage job-rich growth is vital. Additionally, targeted policies to increase FLFP—such as improved childcare support, maternity benefits, and workplace safety—are critical to enhancing workforce inclusivity.

Agricultural Reforms for Rural Transformation

Agriculture continues to employ a significant portion of India's workforce, yet it remains plagued by low productivity and inefficient supply chains. Reforms aimed at improving market access, enhancing irrigation infrastructure, and adopting climate-resilient practices are essential. Expanding farmer access to credit and technology, combined with efforts to reduce post-harvest losses through improved storage and logistics, can further boost rural incomes.

Education and Healthcare: Catalysts for Human Capital Development

Education and healthcare reforms are pivotal to creating a globally competitive workforce. India needs to increase its spending on these sectors, which currently lags behind many peer economies. Initiatives to enhance skill development, strengthen vocational training programs, and improve access to quality healthcare will empower India's youth and boost productivity across sectors.

Digital Revolution and Productivity Gains

India's digital infrastructure, underpinned by initiatives like the Unified Payments Interface (UPI) and the Aadhaar-linked India Stack, has already transformed financial inclusion and governance. These digital platforms are expected to generate significant productivity gains by reducing transaction costs, enhancing service delivery, and fostering innovation across industries. There is a huge potential of digitalization to drive efficiencies in public administration and stimulate entrepreneurship, particularly among micro and small businesses.

Green Transition and Climate Leadership

India's commitment to achieving **net-zero emissions by 2070** represents both a challenge and an opportunity. With the government prioritizing renewable energy and green technologies, investments in solar, wind, and electric vehicles are poised to grow exponentially. India's renewable energy capacity has already surpassed **174 GW**, and ambitious targets such as achieving 500 GW by 2030 signal its leadership in global climate initiatives. To facilitate this transition, India must focus on:

Expanding green financing mechanisms: Encouraging public-private partnerships and leveraging international climate funds.

Scaling sustainable infrastructure projects: Accelerating investments in energy-efficient buildings, smart cities, and clean transportation.

Promoting climate-resilient agriculture: Developing sustainable farming practices to address the risks posed by climate change to food security.

India's financial sector and structural reforms are central to sustaining its growth trajectory and fostering inclusive development. The financial sector's improved resilience reflects effective regulatory oversight, but emerging risks from NBFCs, personal loans, and cooperative banks require proactive management. Simultaneously, structural reforms in labor, agriculture, education, and green energy are crucial to unlocking India's full economic potential. With strategic investments in digital and green transitions, coupled with reforms targeting inclusivity, India is well-positioned to capitalize on its demographic dividend and emerge as a global economic powerhouse.

Key Takeaways for Investors

India's dynamic economic environment, underpinned by robust growth, structural reforms, and global integration, presents substantial opportunities for investors. However, navigating its complexities requires a strategic approach that accounts for evolving risks and opportunities.

Invest in Infrastructure and Green Growth

India's continued emphasis on **infrastructure development** and the **green transition** offers long-term investment opportunities across sectors.

Infrastructure Development: The government's record-high capital expenditure, projected at **3.3% of GDP in FY2023/24**, underscores its commitment to addressing infrastructure gaps in energy, transportation, urban development, and logistics. Initiatives like the **National Infrastructure Pipeline (NIP)** and **PM Gati Shakti** are driving investments in connectivity and supply chain improvements, making India a compelling destination for infrastructure-focused funds.

Renewable Energy: India is spearheading global efforts in renewable energy, aiming to achieve 500 GW of non-fossil fuel capacity by 2030. The transition to green energy, bolstered by supportive policies and international climate finance, opens up investment avenues in solar, wind, and electric vehicle sectors. India's leadership in initiatives like the International Solar Alliance further enhances its attractiveness for sustainable investments.

Monitor Fiscal and Debt Dynamics

Understanding India's fiscal and debt landscape is critical for assessing risks and opportunities, particularly in fixed-income and related sectors.

Fiscal Consolidation Efforts: India's fiscal deficit, projected to decline to 6.0% of GDP in FY2023/24, reflects gradual progress in fiscal consolidation. Investors in government securities should track the government's ability to adhere to its target of 4.5% of GDP by FY2025/26, as this could influence yields and market sentiment.

Debt Management: While India's public debt is high, peaking at **82% of GDP in FY2024/25**, its composition—dominated by long-term, fixed-rate domestic currency debt—mitigates risks. However, contingent liabilities, particularly from the electricity distribution sector, and substantial **gross financing needs (15% of GDP)** remain key areas to monitor.

Policy Stability: India's debt management approach and the importance of maintaining a favorable interest-growth differential is paramount. Investors should assess how government policies and global economic conditions affect borrowing costs and fiscal health.

Leverage Digital Innovation

India's digital transformation, driven by government-backed initiatives, offers unparalleled growth potential across sectors.

Digital Public Infrastructure: Platforms like **Aadhaar**, the **Unified Payments Interface (UPI)**, and the **India Stack** have revolutionized financial inclusion and governance. These innovations provide a strong foundation for startups, fintech companies, and businesses leveraging digital payment systems.

E-Commerce and Technology: India's burgeoning e-commerce market, supported by widespread internet penetration and a young, tech-savvy population, presents opportunities for investors in technology and retail sectors. The growth of digital marketplaces and online services has also accelerated the adoption of cloud computing and AI-driven solutions.

Policy Support: Government programs like **Digital India** and tax incentives for IT and software services further enhance the investment climate in the digital economy.

Diversify to Mitigate Risks

While India offers significant growth potential, its economy is not without risks. Strategic diversification can help investors navigate inflation volatility, external trade uncertainties, and fiscal pressures.

Inflation Volatility: India's headline inflation, projected to average 5.4% in FY2023/24, remains sensitive to food price shocks and global commodity trends. Investors should consider inflation-linked instruments or sectors that perform well during periods of price volatility, such as technology or export-driven industries.

External Trade Risks: The current account deficit (CAD) is expected to narrow to 1.8% of GDP in FY2023/24, but global supply chain disruptions, geopolitical tensions, and fluctuating energy prices could pose challenges. Diversification into export-oriented companies or sectors aligned with resilient markets, like services exports, can mitigate exposure to external shocks.

Fiscal Pressures: Contingent risks from subsidies and public sector inefficiencies are still noticeable. Investors should focus on sectors benefiting from government reforms, such as clean energy, education, and healthcare, while monitoring fiscal risks tied to social spending and subsidies.

India's growth story offers compelling opportunities, particularly in infrastructure, green energy, digital innovation, and export-oriented industries. However, investors must remain vigilant about fiscal dynamics, inflation risks, and external vulnerabilities. A diversified, long-term investment approach, aligned with India's structural reforms and policy priorities, will be key to capitalizing on the country's immense economic potential while mitigating risks.

Chapter conclusion: Navigating the Future: India's Path to Inclusive and Sustainable Growth

India's economic outlook is a dynamic narrative of resilience, opportunity, and reform. As one of the fastest-growing major economies, the country is leveraging its demographic dividend, strategic reforms, and robust investment in infrastructure to propel itself into a position of global leadership. Despite challenges like inflation volatility, fiscal deficits, and external sector vulnerabilities, India has demonstrated remarkable agility in addressing these issues through targeted policy measures, fostering a stable and conducive environment for growth.

Key pillars such as public investment in infrastructure, digital transformation, and the green transition underline India's commitment to sustainable development. The digital economy, supported by government-backed innovations like UPI and Aadhaar, is revolutionizing financial inclusion and service delivery, while the ambitious renewable energy targets are setting the stage for a future-focused economy.

India's fiscal strategy reflects the delicate balancing act of fostering growth while managing debt sustainability. Structural reforms in tax administration, labor markets, agriculture, and human capital development are critical for maintaining momentum. These efforts will not only enhance productivity but also drive inclusivity, ensuring that economic gains are broadly shared across regions and demographics.

Investors have much to gain from India's evolving landscape. Long-term opportunities abound in infrastructure, green energy, and digital innovation. However, a strategic approach is essential to navigate risks tied to fiscal pressures, inflation volatility, and global economic uncertainties. By focusing on diversification and alignment with India's policy priorities, investors can position themselves to capitalize on the country's vast potential.

Looking ahead, India's trajectory is one of optimism and resilience. Its focus on inclusive growth, sustainability, and global integration ensures that it will remain a compelling destination for investment and a key driver of global economic momentum in the decades to come. By continuing its path of strategic reforms and prudent policymaking, India is poised to not only achieve its ambitious economic goals but also inspire confidence as a leading force in the global economy.

Chapter (5)

China's High-Stakes Economic Evolution: Opportunities Amid Structural Risks and Policy Adjustments

"We must work together to build BRICS into a primary channel for strengthening solidarity and cooperation among Global South nations and a vanguard for advancing global governance reform."

Xi Jinping, President of China

China, as a global player, is navigating a transformative economic landscape marked by impressive growth but with complex structural challenges. With a population surpassing 1.4 billion, China holds the distinction of being the most populous country in the world, and its vast expanse of 9.6 million square kilometers makes it the fourth-largest nation by area. Its geography is as diverse as it is extensive, ranging from the towering peaks of the Himalayas, including Mount Everest at 8,849 meters, to the sprawling plains and river deltas in the east. Bordered by 14 countries and with a coastline extending over 14,500 kilometers, China occupies a strategically significant position in East Asia, linking continental and maritime trade routes. It is flanked by the East China Sea, the Yellow Sea, and the South China Sea, with major maritime claims in its exclusive economic zones, highlighting its global economic and geopolitical importance.

The country's terrain includes high plateaus, arid deserts, and fertile lowlands, creating diverse climates that range from tropical in the south to subarctic in the north. This natural diversity has allowed China to harness vast resources, including coal, petroleum, and rare earth elements, while also boasting the world's largest potential for hydropower. Its river systems, including the Yangtze and Yellow Rivers, not only sustain dense population centers but also serve as crucial arteries for agriculture, industry, and trade.

Historically, China's development has been deeply intertwined with its geography and natural resources, enabling it to emerge as a global manufacturing hub and a leader in economic output. Since the late 20th century, China's economy has undergone a remarkable transformation, fueled by market-oriented reforms and integration into global trade networks.

These changes have elevated China to the world's second-largest economy by nominal GDP and the largest in purchasing power parity (PPP). In 2023, China's nominal GDP stood at approximately $17.8 trillion, reflecting its sustained economic expansion over the decades. Measured in PPP terms, China's GDP reached an estimated $31.2 trillion in 2023, solidifying its position as the global leader by this metric. The country's rapid growth trajectory, averaging over 9% annually for much of the late 20th and early 21st centuries, has slowed in recent years as the economy matures and transitions toward high-quality growth.

China's GDP growth rate was 5.2% in 2023 and is projected to maintain a moderate pace of around 5% in 2024. This trajectory reflects ongoing structural reforms, a pivot toward domestic consumption, and investments in high-tech and green industries. While these adjustments signify a gradual deceleration compared to its earlier growth peaks, they align with China's goals of achieving sustainable and innovation-driven economic development in the years ahead.

Yet, the pace of growth has brought with it significant challenges. The real estate sector, plagued by over-leveraging, and local government debt remain key vulnerabilities that have drawn attention from global investors and policymakers alike.

China's demographic distribution further shapes its economic profile. Overwhelmingly concentrated in the eastern half of the country, the population supports thriving urban centers such as Shanghai, Beijing, and Shenzhen. At the same time, vast tracts of the western region remain sparsely populated, dominated by mountains and deserts.

China's strategic role extends beyond its economy. It is a key player in international trade, with seven of the world's ten largest container ports located on its shores. It leads global production in industries ranging from electronics to heavy machinery, while initiatives such as the Belt and Road Initiative underscore its ambitions to shape global connectivity and commerce. However, these advances have been tempered by environmental concerns, including air and water pollution, soil degradation, and a reliance on coal that makes it the world's largest emitter of carbon dioxide.

The International Monetary Fund (IMF) and other global organizations recognize the complexity of China's economic trajectory. Recent policies aimed at stabilizing growth have offered some relief but have not fully addressed long-term structural challenges. For investors and global stakeholders, understanding China's interplay of geographic, demographic, and economic factors is essential to navigating its evolving market landscape. Below, we unpack the unique blend of promise and precariousness that defines China's role in the 21st-century global economy.

Growth Against the Odds: Resilience in a Shifting Economy

China's post-pandemic recovery has showcased the resilience of its economy, despite substantial challenges. As mentioned earlier, supported by strong public investment and a consumption recovery, GDP expanded by 5.2% in 2023 and is expected to grow by 5% in 2024. This robust performance underscores China's ability to leverage its massive industrial base, skilled labor force, and infrastructure capacity. As the world's second-largest economy in nominal terms and the largest in purchasing power parity (PPP), China has relied on targeted fiscal measures and monetary easing to cushion economic shocks. However, the shadow of an ongoing real estate crisis looms. With property market contractions impacting consumer confidence and threatening local government revenue streams, the property sector's recovery remains critical to ensuring broader economic stability.

China's resilience also draws on its unique demographic and geographic strengths. The population of over 1.4 billion, overwhelmingly concentrated in urbanized eastern regions, provides a strong domestic market to support recovery efforts. Urbanization, now at 64.6%, continues to drive demand for housing, services, and infrastructure, even as the property sector undergoes painful corrections. Simultaneously, China's substantial natural resources—including coal, petroleum, and rare earth elements—support its industrial sectors, enabling continued investment in public works and large-scale projects critical to sustaining growth.

Consumer Confidence Amid Structural Drag

A sharp post-pandemic rebound in private consumption, growing at 9% in 2023, has been vital for domestic demand. As China's economy reorients toward a consumption-driven model, stabilizing consumer spending has played a key role in offsetting slower investment growth. With households returning to pre-pandemic saving rates, spending has helped balance structural drags from the ongoing property sector crisis. Nevertheless, the impact of declining property values on household wealth and confidence continues to cast uncertainty on long-term growth. Real estate not only represents a significant share of household assets but also underpins much of local government revenue through land sales—a critical funding mechanism for infrastructure projects.

The consumer market's evolution reflects broader demographic trends. China's population is aging, with 14.4% aged 65 or older, placing pressure on the workforce and social support systems. Yet, a median age of 40.2 years positions China favorably compared to more developed economies, maintaining a strong base of working-age consumers. The country's emphasis on technological adoption and urban middle-class expansion supports sustained growth in private consumption, particularly in technology-driven and service-oriented sectors.

Low Inflation, High Stakes

Persistent disinflationary pressures have characterized China's post-pandemic recovery, with inflation hovering near zero due to subdued domestic demand and low global commodity prices. In 2023, inflation was nearly flat, with consumer prices rising modestly by 0.7% in 2024, as projected by the IMF. While low inflation aids in preserving consumer purchasing power, it also signals economic slack, particularly in industrial production and fixed-asset investment. China's industrial sector, which accounts for over 38% of GDP, faces challenges from weaker global demand and capacity utilization issues.

China's policymakers have responded to these pressures with a mix of fiscal stimulus and monetary easing, aiming to address demand deficiencies while avoiding exacerbation of structural vulnerabilities. The government's focus on supply chain modernization, renewable energy investments, and digital transformation highlights strategic efforts to stimulate growth without relying solely on traditional manufacturing and export-driven models.

Exports Stabilize as Services Grow

China's current account surplus, declining to 1.4% of GDP in 2023, reflects shifts in its trade balance. Rising outbound tourism and adjustments in global demand patterns have impacted the export sector, traditionally a cornerstone of China's economic strength. While exports of electronics, machinery, and textiles remain critical, slower global growth and geopolitical tensions are reshaping China's trade dynamics. Despite these challenges, exports still accounted for nearly 19.7% of GDP in 2023, underscoring their enduring importance in the economy.

Export Landscape

China's export sector remains robust, with total exports valued at approximately $3.511 trillion in 2023. The United States is China's largest export partner, receiving about 15% of its total exports in 2022. Other significant partners include Hong Kong (7%), Japan (5%), Germany (4%), and South Korea (4%). These trade relationships highlight China's integration into global supply chains and its reliance on both advanced and regional economies for market access. Key export categories include:

Broadcasting equipment: A leading category, reflecting China's dominance in high-tech manufacturing.

Integrated circuits: Essential for global electronics industries.

Computers and accessories: Core components of China's technological exports.

Garments and textiles: Representing its strength in traditional manufacturing.

Machine parts: A critical component in global industrial supply chains.

These exports demonstrate China's role as both a supplier of high-value goods and a participant in consumer-oriented sectors.

Import Dynamics

China's imports in 2023 totaled $3.125 trillion, reflecting its status as a major global consumer of goods and raw materials. Key import partners include:

South Korea (7% of imports): Supplies semiconductors and other high-tech components critical to China's electronics industry.

Japan (6%): Provides machinery and automotive products.

Australia (6%): A leading supplier of raw materials, including iron ore and natural gas.

United States (7%): Exports agricultural products, aircraft, and semiconductors to China.

Germany (4%): Supplies machinery and chemicals, reflecting its advanced industrial base. China's key import categories include:

Crude petroleum: A major input for its energy-intensive industries.

Integrated circuits: Vital for maintaining its position in electronics manufacturing.

Iron ore: Fuels its massive construction and manufacturing sectors.

Natural gas: Supports its transition to cleaner energy sources.

Gold: Reflecting its role in the global financial and industrial sectors.

These imports highlight China's reliance on raw materials for its industrial economy and its interconnectedness with global markets for advanced technology.

Infrastructure and Global Connectivity

China's trade dominance is supported by world-class infrastructure, including seven of the world's ten largest container ports, such as Shanghai, Ningbo, and Shenzhen. These facilities handle significant volumes of goods, ensuring efficient trade flows. China's extensive railway and highway networks further strengthen its role as a global logistics hub.

The "Belt and Road Initiative" (BRI) reinforces China's connectivity with trade and investment corridors spanning Asia, Africa, and Europe. While the BRI has bolstered trade volumes and opened new markets, concerns regarding transparency and sustainability remain. These infrastructure investments and trade agreements showcase China's efforts to secure its position as a central player in global trade networks.

Balancing Trade and Economic Rebalancing

China's government continues to emphasize the growth of service industries, which now contribute over 54% of GDP, as part of its rebalancing efforts. Outbound tourism—a reflection of rising incomes and a growing middle class—has seen a resurgence, further balancing trade flows and reducing dependency on merchandise exports. Service exports, including logistics, education, and digital services, complement the country's traditional strengths in goods trade, offering new avenues for economic growth.

Future Outlook

Despite challenges such as slower global demand and geopolitical tensions, China's trade sector remains resilient, underpinned by its infrastructure, diverse industrial base, and global partnerships. As the country shifts toward higher-value manufacturing and green technologies, its trade portfolio is expected to evolve further. With exports of renewable energy technologies, electric vehicles, and advanced machinery growing, China's role in shaping global trade patterns will likely expand, reinforcing its position as an indispensable hub in the international economy.

US tariffs effect, a trade war?

The recent escalation of U.S. tariffs on Chinese imports has cast a wide net, affecting multiple industries and altering trade dynamics between the two economic powerhouses. On 13 September 2024, the United States Trade Representative (USTR) announced the final Section 301 tariff increases on imports from China, following the original proposal in May 2024.

In May 2022, the U.S. Trade Representative (USTR) launched its statutory four-year review of tariff measures, signaling to domestic industries benefiting from these policies the possibility of their termination. This notification also offered industry representatives a critical opportunity to advocate for the continuation of the tariff actions. By September 2022, the USTR confirmed that requests for continuation had been submitted, effectively keeping the tariffs in place while initiating a comprehensive review process.

To facilitate public input, the USTR opened a public docket on November 15, 2022, inviting stakeholders to share their perspectives on various aspects of the review. The response was robust, with nearly 1,500 comments submitted from individuals, organizations, and industry representatives.

Throughout 2023 and into early 2024, the USTR, alongside the Section 301 Committee—a specialized, staff-level group within the interagency Trade Policy Staff Committee (TPSC)—delved into the complex review process. This involved numerous consultations with agency experts to thoroughly analyze the comments received and assess the broader implications of the tariff measures under review. These efforts reflect the depth of scrutiny and stakeholder engagement inherent in shaping U.S. trade policy. Below is an example of the impacted products, the specific tariffs imposed and application date:

Product	Previous tariffs rate	Modieifed tariffs rate	Application date
Battery parts (Non-lithium-Ion)	10%	25%	2024
Electric vehicles	25%	100%	2024
Facemasks	7.5%	25% (2024), 50% (2026)	2024/2026
Lithium-Ion EV Batteries	10%	25%	2024
Lithium-Ion Non-EV Batteries	10%	25%	2026
Medical Gloves	7.5%	50% (2025), 100% (2026)	2025/2026
Natural Graphite	10%	25%	2026
Other Critical Minerals	5%-10%	25%	2024
Permanent Magnets	15%	25%	2026
Semiconductors	25%	50%	2025
Ship-to-Shore Cranes	10%	25%	2024
Solar Cells	25%	50%	2024
Steel & Aluminum	10%-15%	25%	2024

The full list is included in the Section 301 Annex A: Section 301 Modifications Determination FRN (Sept 12 2024) (FINAL).pdf on https://ustr.gov/sites

Electric Vehicles (EVs):

Tariff Increase: From 25% to 100%, effective September 27, 2024.

Impact on Exports: In 2022, China exported approximately $459.3 million worth of EVs to the U.S., which decreased by 27.8% to $331.3 million in 2023. The quadrupling of tariffs is expected to further suppress these figures.

Lithium-Ion Electric Vehicle Batteries:

Tariff Increase: From 7.5% to 25%, effective September 27, 2024.

Impact on Exports: In 2022, China's exports of these batteries to the U.S. were valued at $10.1 billion, rising by 34% to $13.5 billion in 2023. The increased tariffs are anticipated to dampen this growth trajectory.

Solar Cells (Whether or Not Assembled into Modules):

Tariff Increase: From 25% to 50%, effective September 27, 2024.

Impact on Exports: The U.S. imports a significant portion of its solar products from China. The doubling of tariffs is expected to reduce the competitiveness of Chinese solar exports in the U.S. market.

Steel and Aluminum Products:

Tariff Increase: To 25%, effective September 27, 2024 from (0-7.5)%.

Impact on Exports: These tariffs aim to reduce dependency on Chinese imports and address concerns over dumping practices, potentially decreasing Chinese steel and aluminum exports to the U.S.

Semiconductors:

Tariff Increase: From 25% to 50%, effective January 1, 2025.

Medical Products (e.g., Syringes, Needles, Rubber Medical and Surgical Gloves):

Tariff Increase: Up to 100%, with phased implementations between 2024 and 2026.

These tariff adjustments reflect the U.S. administration's strategy to counter perceived unfair trade practices and to bolster domestic industries. The broad scope and significant rates of these tariffs are poised to reshape trade flows, compelling both Chinese exporters and U.S. importers to reassess their supply chain strategies in response to the evolving trade landscape.

The imposition of U.S. tariffs on Chinese goods has woven a complex web of economic and trade dynamics, sending ripples across the global marketplace. The effects have been both immediate and long-term, influencing China's domestic economy, altering trade flows, and reshaping the contours of globalization.

Impact on China's Economy:

A Race Against Tariffs: Anticipating punitive tariffs, Chinese exporters scrambled to push goods overseas. In late 2024, exports surged by an impressive 10.7%, defying expectations and highlighting the frenetic pace of pre-emptive trade. Major markets such as the United States, the European Union, and

Southeast Asia all saw a flood of Chinese products, as manufacturers sought to outpace the tariffs' implementation.

Booming Trade Surplus Amid Challenges: Despite these headwinds, China recorded a historic trade surplus of nearly $1 trillion in 2024, a figure that underscores its pivotal role in global trade. Yet, this milestone carries a shadow. The surplus has drawn fire from the United States and other nations, fuelling accusations of unfair trade practices and intensifying calls for protectionist measures.

Navigating Economic Crosswinds: Domestically, the tariffs have tested China's economic resilience. Growth, while meeting the government's modest target of 5%, has been underpinned by aggressive fiscal policies and strategic stimulus measures. Concerns about deflation and tepid consumer demand have driven Beijing to consider even bolder interventions to keep its economic engines humming.

Impact on Trade Relations:

A Global Tilt Toward Protectionism: The U.S. tariffs on Chinese goods have acted as a spark, igniting a wave of protectionism worldwide. Countries from Brazil to Indonesia have joined the fray, imposing barriers on Chinese imports. The global stage, once marked by aspirations of free trade, now finds itself embroiled in rising walls of tariffs and quotas.

Shifts in Trade Patterns: As the trade environment grows increasingly fraught, countries are recalibrating their strategies. For instance, nations like Vietnam and Mexico have emerged as alternative manufacturing hubs, benefiting from the shift of supply chains away from China. While some economies adapt and thrive, the overall effect on global trade has been a chilling slowdown.

Warning Bells from the IMF: The International Monetary Fund has sounded alarms about the broader consequences of escalating trade disputes. Projections indicate that a sustained increase in tariffs could erode global economic output by up to 1.3% by 2026. This contraction would undermine not only China but also the interconnected economies dependent on stable trade flows.

Broader Implications:

Reshaping the Rules of Trade: The U.S.-China trade tensions have forced a rethinking of globalization. Companies, wary of sudden policy shifts, are diversifying their supply chains, investing in regional markets, and reevaluating dependencies on single nations. This de-globalization trend could create more resilient but fragmented trade networks.

Strained Bilateral Relations: At the heart of this economic clash lies a deeper geopolitical rivalry. The tariffs are as much a reflection of economic strategy as they are of ideological divergence. For China, the challenge is to assert its growing economic might while navigating a more confrontational international landscape.

At the same time, the U.S. tariffs on Chinese goods have done more than disrupt trade; they have acted as a catalyst for a profound transformation of global economic relations. China's economy, though resilient, faces mounting challenges as it adapts to a world less welcoming of its dominance. Meanwhile, the global economy grapples with the tension between interdependence and self-preservation. This ongoing saga underscores a pivotal truth: in an interconnected world, no nation, however powerful, operates in isolation.

Debt Dynamics and Fiscal Adjustments: Tackling Local Government Strains

China's fiscal strategy must balance the need to support economic growth with the heavy debt burdens weighing on local governments. As the country grapples with the dual challenges of slowing property market revenues and increasing demands for infrastructure investment, fiscal reforms remain a key priority. The IMF underscores the necessity of sustained structural adjustments to address these pressures, particularly as local government financing vehicles (LGFVs) play an increasingly prominent role in borrowing.

Local Government Debt: The Hidden Risk

With local government debt levels, including LGFVs, estimated to be equivalent to 124% of GDP, China's debt burden has become a critical concern. Much of this debt is tied to infrastructure development, land sales, and other investments aimed at spurring economic activity. However, the downturn in the property sector—historically a key revenue source—has severely limited local governments' financial flexibility. This decline not only affects their ability to fund projects but also weakens revenue streams from property taxes and land lease sales.

Regional disparities exacerbate the issue. While economically advanced provinces like Guangdong and Jiangsu maintain stronger fiscal positions due to diversified revenue bases, less developed western provinces with sparse populations and lower economic activity struggle to manage debt obligations. Supply-side initiatives such as affordable housing development and tax incentives for technological innovation have further strained local budgets, forcing many governments to rely on central support and debt restructuring.

China's geography and population distribution contribute to these challenges. The eastern provinces, densely populated and urbanized, dominate economic activity, while vast western regions face limited fiscal capacity due to their sparse populations and challenging terrain. Additional central government support and fiscal restructuring measures may be necessary to prevent local financial crises that could disrupt broader economic stability.

Easing Policy for Strategic Growth

Amid these fiscal strains, the People's Bank of China (PBOC) has employed monetary easing measures, including lowering reserve requirements and cutting interest rates, to stimulate demand and counteract disinflationary pressures. This approach is aimed at alleviating economic slack while supporting credit flow to critical sectors such as manufacturing and technology. However, the financial difficulties of local governments could complicate the effectiveness of these policies, as heavily indebted regions may struggle to absorb new investments or repay existing obligations.

It is recommended that China continue its accommodative monetary policies while adopting greater exchange rate flexibility to manage external pressures. This strategy aligns with China's broader economic goals, which include promoting exports, encouraging domestic consumption, and supporting emerging industries such as renewable energy and high-tech manufacturing.

A New Fiscal Strategy

China's 2024 budget reflected a shift toward a more balanced fiscal approach, with special bonds allocated for strategic investments in digital infrastructure, renewable energy, and other high-priority areas. By earmarking funds for green and technological advancements, the government aims to foster long-term economic transformation while curbing unsustainable debt accumulation.

This cautious but forward-looking stance illustrates Beijing's intention to strike a delicate balance between fiscal discipline and growth promotion. By focusing on targeted investments in innovation and sustainability, the government hopes to stimulate economic development while mitigating risks from high debt levels. Additionally, China's extensive natural resources and industrial capacity provide opportunities to align these strategic investments with global trends in decarbonization and digitalization, reinforcing its economic resilience.

Outlook on Debt and Fiscal Reform

China's debt dynamics and fiscal policy remain pivotal to its economic trajectory. The challenges posed by declining property market revenues, uneven regional development, and mounting local government debt require a multi-pronged strategy that includes central government intervention, fiscal restructuring, and strategic investment in high-growth sectors. As China navigates these complexities, the success of its fiscal adjustments will likely determine the stability of its broader economic model in the years to come.

The Green Horizon: China's Race to Lead in Renewable Energy and Innovation

Despite fiscal and structural challenges, China's commitment to a green economy and technological innovation presents compelling growth opportunities. As the world's largest emitter of carbon dioxide, China recognizes the need to balance its economic ambitions with environmental sustainability. China's significant investments in renewable energy, green technologies, and digital infrastructure underscore its ambitions to emerge as a global leader in sustainable development and innovation.

Clean Energy and Emissions Reduction

China's green transformation is underpinned by its status as the world's largest producer and consumer of renewable energy. Hydropower, solar, and wind energy together account for over 28% of the country's installed electricity generation capacity. China is home to the world's largest hydropower projects, such as the Three Gorges Dam, and has rapidly scaled up its solar and wind energy production to meet ambitious climate goals. In 2022, renewable energy projects continued to expand, with solar and wind accounting for a growing share of its energy mix.

To combat its reliance on coal, China is also focusing on energy efficiency and emissions trading schemes. The country has implemented the world's largest carbon market, covering sectors responsible for the majority of its emissions. By incentivizing reductions through emissions permits and penalties, China is aligning its industrial policies with global climate targets. Moreover, its Belt and Road Initiative is increasingly incorporating green infrastructure projects, offering opportunities for international collaboration in clean energy investments. These initiatives not only aim to reduce China's carbon footprint but also position it as a critical player in global environmental governance.

Innovation-Driven Economy

China's strategic pivot toward high-tech industries reflects its ambition to lead the Fourth Industrial Revolution. The government's focus on developing artificial intelligence (AI), quantum computing, cloud technologies, and next-generation manufacturing highlights its commitment to a digitally-driven economy. Supported by state-backed infrastructure initiatives, China now has the world's largest broadband network and is a global leader in 5G technology deployment, offering a strong foundation for digital innovation.

Beijing has prioritized investments in research and development, allocating substantial funding to foster advancements in biotechnology, robotics, and semiconductor manufacturing. The country's digital economy already accounts for a significant share of its GDP, and initiatives such as smart cities, autonomous vehicles, and green technologies are expected to further accelerate growth. Additionally, China's extensive patent filings and dominance in international tech manufacturing underline its capacity to shape global standards in hardware and software innovations.

Revitalizing Manufacturing

China's manufacturing sector is undergoing a fundamental shift from low-value, labor-intensive production to high-value, technology-driven industries. Its dominance in industries such as electric vehicles (EVs), advanced robotics, and aerospace highlights the evolution of its industrial base. The government's "Made in China 2025" initiative aims to modernize its manufacturing capabilities, making China a leader in high-tech exports.

This shift is supported by the country's abundant natural resources, skilled labor force, and integrated supply chains. China remains a global leader in the production of rare earth elements, critical for technologies ranging from renewable energy to consumer electronics. As global supply chains evolve in response to geopolitical pressures, China's focus on self-reliance in key technologies positions it as a resilient and adaptable manufacturing hub.

Opportunities for Investors

For investors, the green and high-tech sectors present significant opportunities. China's robust renewable energy infrastructure and its commitment to reducing carbon emissions create an attractive environment for investments in green technologies and environmental innovation. Similarly, the country's advances in digital infrastructure and strategic focus on high-value manufacturing offer promising areas for long-term growth.

As the global economy increasingly prioritizes sustainability and technological innovation, China's dual focus on green energy and digital transformation ensures its relevance as a global economic powerhouse. By aligning its domestic policies with global environmental and technological trends, China is poised to lead in shaping the future of both sustainability and innovation.

Real Estate Reset: A Double-Edged Sword for Growth

China's real estate sector remains a significant point of vulnerability, representing a critical yet precarious pillar of the country's economy. With the sector historically accounting for a substantial share of GDP, the persistent challenges of high unsold inventories, cash-strapped developers, and reluctant buyers cast a long shadow on broader economic stability. The IMF underscores the urgency of resolving these imbalances, emphasizing that unchecked turmoil in the real estate market could ripple across local government finances, banking systems, and consumer confidence, endangering overall growth.

Housing Market Correction

China's housing market is undergoing a painful but necessary correction. Residential investment has seen continuous declines, reflecting waning buyer demand and oversupply. The slump in new housing construction remains a key issue, with no clear bottom in sight. Meanwhile, the completion of unfinished housing projects has become a pressing financial and social challenge. The IMF estimates that resolving this backlog alone could cost around 5.5% of GDP over four years, highlighting the significant fiscal burden this poses.

Policy adjustments aimed at stabilizing the sector, including interest rate cuts and easing mortgage conditions, have provided some relief. However, these measures risk delaying a comprehensive resolution and could exacerbate future fiscal costs. The structural overhang of unsold properties reflects deeper issues of speculative investment, misaligned supply and demand, and a dependence on property sales for local government revenues.

Geographically, the crisis is most acute in smaller cities, where population growth is stagnant, and housing demand is limited. By contrast, major urban centers such as Beijing, Shanghai, and Guangzhou have fared relatively better, buoyed by sustained economic activity and population inflows. However, even in these regions, affordability concerns and declining buyer confidence are weighing on market dynamics.

High Developer Distress

The distress in China's real estate sector is amplified by the financial struggles of developers. Despite government measures to inject liquidity and ease refinancing pressures, nearly 50% of developers face severe solvency concerns, with an additional 15% grappling with liquidity challenges. High-profile defaults by major firms have further shaken confidence in the sector. This developer distress has significant downstream effects, including financial strains for local governments heavily reliant on land sales and banks with substantial exposure to real estate loans.

The situation is particularly dire in regions where local governments depend heavily on land lease revenues to fund infrastructure and social programs. With property markets stagnating, these revenue streams are drying up, placing further pressure on public finances. Local government financing vehicles (LGFVs), already burdened by debt, face additional risks from their exposure to struggling developers, creating a feedback loop of fiscal vulnerability.

Balancing Risk and Demand

In response to these challenges, the government has introduced measures such as interest rate reductions, mortgage flexibility, and tax incentives to stimulate housing demand. While these initiatives have provided some short-term relief, the underlying structural issues in the market persist. Restoring buyer confidence remains critical, and experts suggest that allowing market-driven price adjustments could help align supply with actual demand.

The IMF advocates for a comprehensive approach to stabilize the real estate sector. This includes targeted fiscal resources to address housing overhangs, policies to ensure the completion of stalled projects, and strategies to support distressed developers. The development of affordable housing and alternative revenue streams for local governments are also seen as essential to reducing reliance on speculative property sales.

Outlook on the Real Estate Sector

China's real estate reset represents both a challenge and an opportunity. On the one hand, it poses risks to financial stability and economic growth; on the other, it offers a chance to transition toward a more sustainable housing market. By addressing structural imbalances and implementing targeted reforms, China can mitigate risks while fostering a more resilient real estate sector that supports long-term economic stability.

Navigating the Financial Landscape: Stability Amidst Elevated Risks

China's financial sector has demonstrated remarkable resilience, navigating the challenges posed by a slowing economy, global financial volatility, and domestic structural issues. Yet vulnerabilities persist, particularly among smaller banks and nonbank financial institutions, as well as in the interconnected sectors of real estate and local government financing. It is undeniable that unresolved credit risks, stemming from rising nonperforming loans (NPLs) in the property sector and mounting liabilities in local government financing vehicles (LGFVs), could destabilize financial markets and hinder economic recovery.

Banking Sector Resilience

China's banking system is a cornerstone of its financial stability, with major state-owned banks maintaining robust capitalization and steady profitability. These institutions have benefited from strong regulatory oversight and government support, enabling them to weather economic disruptions. However, smaller and rural banks, which account for a significant portion of China's banking sector, face mounting challenges.

These challenges are particularly acute for banks with high exposure to the real estate sector. The downturn in property markets has increased NPLs, straining the balance sheets of banks reliant on real estate-related income. Additionally, rural banks, which often serve less affluent regions, struggle with limited capital buffers, weaker profitability, and higher credit risks. Regional disparities exacerbate these vulnerabilities, as banks in less developed western provinces face greater difficulties compared to their counterparts in eastern economic hubs like Shanghai and Shenzhen.

To address these risks, regulatory reforms have been introduced, including measures to bolster capital adequacy, improve risk management, and enhance governance in smaller banks. The government has also encouraged mergers and acquisitions among weaker institutions to strengthen their resilience. Despite these efforts, the IMF emphasizes the need for comprehensive crisis management frameworks to prevent systemic risks, especially as global financial conditions tighten.

Corporate and Household Debt

China's financial stability is further complicated by elevated debt levels across corporate and household sectors. Corporate debt, estimated at 122% of GDP, remains among the highest globally, reflecting decades of credit-fueled growth. Much of this debt is concentrated in state-owned enterprises (SOEs) and sectors with excess capacity, such as steel and coal. These industries face structural inefficiencies and profitability challenges, increasing the risk of defaults.

Household debt, while lower than corporate debt at approximately 60% of GDP, has risen rapidly in recent years, driven by mortgage borrowing and consumer credit expansion.

The ongoing correction in the property market has amplified risks, as declining property values erode household wealth and confidence, potentially constraining future spending. This dynamic poses a double-edged sword for the economy, as household consumption has become an increasingly important driver of growth.

Targeted measures to mitigate debt risks are recommended, including fiscal support for struggling sectors, stricter enforcement of bankruptcy laws to restructure unviable companies, and policies to stabilize the property market. Additionally, promoting alternative financing channels, such as equity markets and private capital, could reduce reliance on debt-driven growth.

Financial System Reforms

As China's financial landscape evolves, strengthening oversight and transparency in banking and nonbank financial institutions will be critical. Nonbank entities, including asset managers and shadow banking activities, have grown significantly, increasing the complexity and interconnectedness of the financial system. While these institutions play a vital role in diversifying financing channels, their opacity and regulatory gaps pose significant risks.

Regulators have made strides in improving risk oversight, including the establishment of a financial stability and development committee to coordinate supervision across sectors. Efforts to reduce shadow banking activities, enhance disclosure requirements, and strengthen the capital buffers of asset managers are ongoing. However, there is a clear need for a more coordinated strategy to manage potential spillovers from nonbank financial institutions.

Small and regional banks remain a priority for reform, given their vulnerabilities and systemic importance in supporting local economies. Measures such as increasing deposit insurance coverage, enhancing resolution frameworks, and encouraging consolidation among weaker banks could provide stability. Additionally, fostering a culture of accountability and governance reform within financial institutions will be essential to rebuilding public trust and ensuring long-term resilience.

Outlook for Financial Stability

China's financial system stands at a crossroads, balancing the need for stability with the pressures of economic transition. Resolving vulnerabilities in the banking sector, managing corporate and household debt, and reforming nonbank financial institutions are essential to safeguarding financial stability. By strengthening regulatory oversight, enhancing transparency, and adopting a coordinated approach to risk management, China can mitigate financial risks while supporting its broader economic goals.

Despite these challenges, the resilience of China's financial system, coupled with its proactive regulatory measures, positions the country to navigate the evolving financial landscape. For global investors and policymakers, understanding China's financial dynamics is critical to assessing its role in the broader global economy.

Key Takeaways for Strategic Investment in China

China's economic landscape presents a mix of high rewards and elevated risks for investors. As the world's second-largest economy and a global leader in green energy, advanced manufacturing, and digital innovation, China offers substantial opportunities. However, fiscal imbalances, structural vulnerabilities, and evolving regulatory frameworks necessitate a cautious and informed approach. By understanding the country's priorities in green growth, digital transformation, and structural reform, investors can strategically navigate its dynamic economy.

Invest in Sustainability and High-Tech Innovation

China's commitment to sustainability and technological advancement positions its green and digital sectors as prime areas for investment. As the world's largest producer of renewable energy, China is scaling up its wind, solar, and hydropower capacity, with the government targeting carbon neutrality by 2060. These ambitious goals are backed by policies such as subsidies for renewable projects, the expansion of its carbon market, and incentives for green technologies.

The digital economy, another priority, has grown rapidly, fueled by state-led initiatives to expand 5G networks, smart cities, and digital infrastructure. Sectors such as artificial intelligence (AI), cloud computing, and advanced manufacturing receive strong government support, reflecting China's ambition to lead in the Fourth Industrial Revolution. Companies involved in these sectors, especially those aligned with national strategic priorities, are poised to benefit from favorable policies and financing.

For investors, opportunities abound in areas like electric vehicles (EVs), battery technology, clean energy manufacturing, and software and hardware innovations. China's dominance in rare earth elements and its robust manufacturing capacity further bolster its green and tech ambitions, offering significant potential for returns in these high-growth industries.

Monitor Fiscal and Monetary Adjustments

China's balancing act between promoting growth and managing its debt burden remains a central dynamic for investors. Fiscal policies are increasingly focused on targeted spending in strategic sectors, such as renewable energy and high-tech infrastructure, while maintaining a cautious approach to broader public investment. Measures to address the debt challenges of local governments and the property sector could impact liquidity and credit availability in other parts of the economy.

Monetary policy, shaped by the People's Bank of China (PBOC), has remained accommodative, with interest rate cuts and reduced reserve requirements aimed at stimulating demand. However, the effectiveness of these measures may vary across sectors, particularly in areas like real estate and banking, where structural issues persist. Investors should closely monitor fiscal adjustments, such as the allocation of special bonds for strategic investments, and monetary shifts, including exchange rate policies, as these could influence asset values and sectoral growth.

Adopt a Diversified, Long-Term Strategy

China's ongoing structural transitions and policy reforms underscore the importance of a diversified investment strategy. The country's shift from low-value manufacturing to high-value industries offers dynamic opportunities in advanced manufacturing and resilient supply chains. At the same time, its focus on green energy and digital transformation provides new avenues for growth in emerging industries.

Diversifying across these sectors can help mitigate risks associated with China's fiscal and structural uncertainties. For example, green energy investments can capitalize on government incentives and global decarbonization trends, while high-tech innovation offers exposure to rapidly growing digital markets. Manufacturing investments, particularly in export-oriented and supply chain-resilient industries, remain attractive, as China continues to modernize its industrial base.

Long-term investors should also consider regional differences within China. Eastern provinces, with their dense populations and economic hubs, present strong growth opportunities, while western and central regions may require a more nuanced approach due to their slower development. Understanding these regional dynamics and aligning investments with national priorities, such as the Belt and Road Initiative and domestic consumption growth, can enhance portfolio performance.

China's economic trajectory reflects both immense potential and significant challenges. By focusing on sustainability, innovation, and structural reform, investors can identify growth opportunities while navigating risks. Staying informed about fiscal and monetary policies, adopting a diversified approach, and aligning with China's strategic priorities are essential for leveraging the rewards of its evolving economy. For those prepared to engage with its complexity, China remains a pivotal market with the capacity to shape global investment trends in the decades to come.

China's Path to High-Quality Growth: A Dual Challenge of Innovation and Reform

China stands at a pivotal juncture as it transitions from a model driven by rapid industrialization and export-led growth to one that prioritizes sustainability, innovation, and high-quality development. This ambitious shift reflects both its remarkable economic resilience and the pressing need to address structural challenges such as debt, demographic shifts, and environmental pressures. For investors, this dual challenge presents both opportunities and complexities, requiring a nuanced understanding of the evolving landscape.

Balancing Sustainability and Structural Reform

China's commitment to sustainability, evidenced by its aggressive renewable energy investments and ambitious carbon neutrality goals, underscores its long-term growth potential. The country's role as the world's largest producer of renewable energy and a leader in green technology innovation positions it as a critical player in global decarbonization efforts. This focus on sustainability is complemented by its strategic pivot toward high-tech industries, which are driving advancements in areas such as artificial intelligence, quantum computing, and next-generation manufacturing.

However, these opportunities are tempered by significant structural hurdles. The real estate sector remains a source of vulnerability, with high unsold inventories, developer distress, and declining local government revenues creating a feedback loop of economic strain. Similarly, the mounting debt levels among corporations, households, and local governments pose risks that could challenge fiscal stability and slow the pace of reform. Addressing these issues will require a careful balancing act between promoting growth and ensuring financial discipline.

Resilience Through Reform and Innovation

China's resilience lies in its ability to adapt and reform. Policies aimed at strengthening the banking sector, reducing reliance on debt-driven growth, and fostering regional development are indicative of its proactive approach. These reforms, coupled with strategic investments in digital infrastructure, advanced manufacturing, and clean energy, offer pathways to overcome short-term challenges and build a more sustainable economy.

For investors, the key lies in identifying sectors aligned with China's long-term priorities. Opportunities abound in green energy, digital innovation, and advanced manufacturing, where government support and global trends intersect to create high-growth potential. At the same time, a diversified approach that accounts for sectoral and regional variations can help mitigate risks associated with China's structural transitions.

Chapter Conclusion: Engaging in a Dynamic Market

China remains one of the world's most dynamic and influential markets. Its sheer scale, combined with its rapid pace of technological advancement and commitment to sustainability, ensures its continued relevance on the global stage. However, the complexity of its economic transformation necessitates a cautious and informed approach. Investors must remain attuned to policy shifts, regulatory changes, and market dynamics, particularly in vulnerable sectors such as real estate and local government finance.

While the path to high-quality growth is not without challenges, China's trajectory offers a compelling narrative of resilience and reform. For those prepared to navigate its complexities, China represents a unique opportunity to engage in a market where innovation, sustainability, and structural reform converge to shape the future of the global economy.

Chapter (6)

South Africa: Balancing Economic Promise with Structural Challenges

"BRICS has an important role in the world. It has the potential to drive significant change in the global economy and international relations"

Cyril Ramaphosa, President of South Africa

South Africa stands at a unique crossroads as a country of immense economic potential and significant challenges. Situated at the southernmost tip of Africa, it shares borders with six countries: Botswana, Lesotho (which it entirely surrounds), Mozambique, Namibia, Eswatini (almost completely surrounded), and Zimbabwe. Its vast geography encompasses 1,219,090 square kilometers, including the Prince Edward Islands, making it slightly less than twice the size of Texas. South Africa is strategically positioned with a 2,798-kilometer coastline along the Atlantic and Indian Oceans, providing access to vital global trade routes.

The country's terrain is diverse, comprising a vast interior plateau rimmed by rugged hills and narrow coastal plains. Its climate varies from semiarid to subtropical along the east coast, with sunny days and cool nights. This diverse geography supports rich biodiversity and makes South Africa a key player in global conservation efforts, with 12 UNESCO World Heritage Sites showcasing its natural and cultural treasures.

With a population of over 60.4 million as of 2024, South Africa is the 25th most populous country globally. Its demographic profile reveals a youthful nation gradually aging, with a median age of 30.4 years. However, high unemployment, especially among the youth (49.1%), reflects systemic economic challenges. The population is concentrated along the southern and southeastern coasts and inland around major cities like Pretoria, Johannesburg, and Cape Town. Urbanization is a defining trend, with 68.8% of the population residing in urban areas, a figure that continues to grow annually by 1.72%.

Ethnically, South Africa is a melting pot, with Black Africans comprising 80.9% of the population, followed by Colored (8.8%), White (7.8%), and Indian/Asian (2.6%) groups. This diversity is mirrored in its linguistic landscape, with 11 official languages, including isiZulu, isiXhosa, and Afrikaans, alongside English, which serves as a unifying language in government and commerce.

Despite its challenges, South Africa boasts Africa's largest stock exchange and a diverse industrial base supported by an abundance of natural resources, including gold, platinum, coal, and diamonds. Yet, stark income inequality, evidenced by a Gini index of 63, and systemic issues such as poor utilities management hinder its economic potential. For investors, South Africa represents a land of contrasts—rich in opportunities yet fraught with risks that demand careful navigation of its dynamic economic and regulatory landscape.

Economic Overview: A Mixed Landscape

South Africa's economy, classified as upper-middle-income, has been shaped by its rich history, extensive natural resource base, and significant industrial capacity. However, it also faces a range of structural challenges, including inefficient utilities management, high unemployment, income inequality, and subdued economic growth. These factors create a complex economic environment that offers both opportunities and risks for investors.

GDP Dynamics

The real GDP in 2023 stood at $862.981 billion (PPP), with a modest annual growth rate of 0.6%, reflecting a slowing economy following a strong post-COVID recovery period in 2021 and 2022. This decline in growth is attributed to persistent challenges, such as high inflation (6.07% in 2023), unreliable energy supply, and external pressures on exports. Despite this, South Africa remains the 33rd largest economy globally in terms of purchasing power parity, underscoring its significance as a key economic player in Africa.

Sectoral Contributions

The structure of South Africa's economy highlights the dominance of services, which contributed 63% of GDP in 2023. This sector is driven by financial services, telecommunications, and retail trade, reflecting a modern, urbanized economy. Industry, including mining, manufacturing, and construction, accounts for 24.6% of GDP, while agriculture contributes a modest 2.5%. Despite its small share, agriculture remains vital for rural livelihoods and food security, with top products including sugarcane, maize, and grapes. The underutilized potential of the agricultural sector, coupled with the need for modernization in farming practices, represents a promising avenue for future investment.

Labor Market

South Africa's labor market is one of its most pressing challenges. The unemployment rate remains among the highest globally at 27.99% in 2023, with youth unemployment reaching an alarming 49.1%. This disproportionate impact on younger populations highlights a critical need for targeted job creation strategies, particularly in emerging industries such as technology and renewable energy. The country's labor force of 25.158 million reflects its large pool of potential workers, yet systemic issues such as skills mismatches, weak education outcomes, and limited economic diversification hinder progress.

Inequality and Social Challenges

Despite being Africa's most industrialized nation, South Africa grapples with deep-seated inequality that permeates its social and economic fabric. These disparities are the result of historical injustices, structural economic inefficiencies, and uneven access to resources and opportunities.

Gini Index: A Measure of Inequality

South Africa consistently ranks as one of the most unequal countries in the world. With a Gini index score of 63 (2014), it leads global measurements of income inequality:

Disparities in Wealth: The top 10% of income earners control over 50.5% of total income, while the bottom 10% receive just 0.9%.

Historical Legacy: The legacy of apartheid continues to influence the distribution of wealth and opportunities, with Black South Africans disproportionately represented among the poor.

Geographic Inequality: Rural areas are particularly affected by poverty and lack of services, while urban centers see significant income disparities between affluent suburbs and informal settlements.

Poverty: A National Crisis

More than 55.5% of South Africa's population lives below the national poverty line, with widespread implications for social stability and economic growth:

Rural Poverty: Rural regions face higher poverty rates due to limited access to education, healthcare, and employment opportunities.

Children in Poverty: High poverty levels disproportionately affect children, exacerbating cycles of poor education, malnutrition, and limited future opportunities.

Healthcare and Nutrition: Persistent poverty contributes to poor health outcomes, with many families unable to afford adequate healthcare or balanced nutrition.

Urbanization: Opportunities and Strains

With 68.8% of the population living in urban areas as of 2023, urbanization is both an opportunity and a challenge:

Housing Pressure: Rapid urban growth has led to the proliferation of informal settlements where millions live without adequate access to basic services such as water, electricity, and sanitation.

Infrastructure Strain: Urban centers face overstretched infrastructure, including transportation, healthcare facilities, and schools, struggling to keep pace with population growth.

Employment Concentration: While cities like Johannesburg and Cape Town offer more job opportunities, high urban unemployment remains a critical issue, particularly among the youth.

Education and Skills Gaps

Education, a vital lever for reducing inequality, faces challenges in South Africa:

Quality Gaps: While literacy rates are relatively high at 95%, the quality of education remains uneven, with rural and township schools often underfunded and poorly equipped.

Access to Higher Education: Although more students are entering tertiary institutions, many drop out due to financial pressures or inadequate preparation from the basic education system.

Unemployment: An Amplifier of Inequality

Unemployment exacerbates inequality, with 27.99% of the labor force unemployed in 2023:

Youth Unemployment: At 49.1%, the youth unemployment rate is among the highest globally, reflecting systemic issues in education and the job market.

Gender Disparities: Women face higher unemployment rates and are often confined to lower-paying and informal jobs.

Social Challenges and Public Services

South Africa's inequality is mirrored in its uneven access to public services:

Healthcare Access: Although 96.7% of the population has access to improved drinking water sources, healthcare infrastructure remains under strain, with a physician density of only 0.79 per 1,000 people (2019).

Sanitation: While 93.2% of the population has access to improved sanitation, rural areas still lag behind urban centers.

Rich in Resources, Struggling in Distribution

South Africa is renowned for its abundant natural resources, which have historically driven its economic development. These resources provide a foundation for growth and export revenues but are accompanied by significant challenges in distribution, management, and sustainability.

Mining: A Global Leader with Domestic Challenges

South Africa's mining sector is one of its most critical industries and a major player in global markets:

Platinum Leader: The country is the world's largest producer of platinum, a key component in catalytic converters, jewelry, and electronics.

Chromium and Gold: South Africa was the world's leading producer of chromite ore in 2022, with an output of 18,000 metric tons, and remains a significant global producer of gold.

Diverse Minerals: The country is also rich in coal, diamonds, manganese, vanadium, uranium, and rare earth elements.

However, despite these strengths, South Africa faces notable challenges:

Labor Disputes: Strikes and labor unrest frequently disrupt mining operations, reflecting unresolved tensions over wages and working conditions.

Infrastructure Inefficiencies: The industry struggles with aging equipment and transportation bottlenecks, reducing competitiveness and raising operational costs.

Agriculture: Modest Contribution, Vital Importance

Agriculture contributes 2.5% to South Africa's GDP but remains vital for food security and exports:

Key Crops: The country's agricultural outputs include sugarcane, maize, milk, potatoes, and wheat. High-value fruits like grapes, oranges, and apples also play a significant role in both domestic markets and exports.

Land Use: Of the country's total land area, 79.4% is classified as agricultural land. However, only 9.9% is arable, while 69.2% is permanent pasture, emphasizing reliance on extensive farming methods.

Challenges in agriculture include:

Water Scarcity: With an irrigated land area of just 16,700 square kilometers, water-intensive crops face risks from prolonged droughts and increasing water demand across sectors.

Sustainability Issues: Soil erosion, desertification, and land degradation remain persistent problems, threatening long-term agricultural productivity.

Energy: Reliance on Coal and the Path to Renewables

South Africa's energy sector is heavily reliant on fossil fuels, with coal dominating its electricity generation:

Coal Dependency: In 2022, 87.8% of the country's installed electricity capacity was derived from coal, reflecting the importance of this resource for both domestic consumption and exports.

Production and Trade: South Africa produced 245.467 million metric tons of coal in 2022, exporting 75.512 million metric tons while consuming 176.148 million metric tons domestically.

Efforts to diversify the energy mix have begun:

Renewable Energy: Wind and solar energy together accounted for just 6.9% of installed capacity in 2022, highlighting the slow pace of the energy transition.

Nuclear Contribution: South Africa's two nuclear reactors provided 4.4% of its total electricity generation, with a net capacity of 1.85 GW.

Challenges in the energy sector include:

Infrastructure Failures: Chronic mismanagement and technical issues at state-owned utility Eskom have led to frequent power outages, undermining economic growth and investor confidence.

Carbon Emissions: South Africa emitted 476.987 million metric tons of CO2 in 2022, with coal and metallurgical coke contributing 392.305 million metric tons.

Struggles in Distribution and Management

Despite its resource wealth, South Africa faces systemic challenges in distribution and resource management:

Infrastructure Bottlenecks: A lack of investment in modernizing mining and energy infrastructure reduces efficiency and hampers economic output.

Inequality in Benefits: The wealth generated by resource industries is not equitably distributed, with rural areas particularly lagging in development and access to services.

Toward a Sustainable Future

Addressing these challenges will require comprehensive reforms and strategic investments:

Accelerating Renewables: Expanding the role of renewable energy sources can reduce reliance on coal and contribute to sustainability goals.

Modernizing Agriculture: Investing in sustainable farming practices and water management is critical to safeguarding agricultural productivity.

Inclusive Growth: Ensuring equitable resource distribution through policy reforms and infrastructure investments is essential for long-term social and economic stability.

South Africa's vast natural resource base remains a cornerstone of its economy, offering substantial opportunities for growth and diversification. However, unlocking this potential requires overcoming entrenched challenges and embracing a sustainable, inclusive approach to development.

Trade and Investment

South Africa's trade and investment landscape is deeply intertwined with its rich natural resources and industrial capacity, positioning the country as a vital player in regional and global markets. Its trade profile reflects its diverse economy and strategic geographic location.

Exports: Resource and Industrial Powerhouse

South Africa's export profile is dominated by its rich mineral resources and manufactured goods:

Key Export Commodities: Gold, platinum, coal, diamonds, and automobiles are among the top export items, reflecting the country's dual strength in resource extraction and industrial production.

Export Markets:

China: South Africa's largest trading partner, accounting for 16% of total exports in 2022, benefits primarily from its imports of minerals and metals.

United States and Germany: Each accounted for 7% of South Africa's exports in 2022, with automobiles and mineral products forming the backbone of these trade relationships.

India and Japan: Represent 6% each of export markets, with growing demand for South Africa's coal and other raw materials.

In 2023, total exports were valued at $124.731 billion, reflecting South Africa's role as a leading exporter in key sectors.

Imports: Critical Goods for Development

South Africa relies on imports to sustain its industrial base and meet domestic consumption needs:

Key Import Commodities: Refined petroleum, cars, vehicle parts, and broadcasting equipment are significant imports, supporting energy needs and the automotive industry. Top Suppliers:

China: Dominates South Africa's import market with 21% of total imports in 2022, driven by machinery, electronics, and other industrial goods.

Germany: Contributes 9%, providing vehicles, industrial machinery, and pharmaceuticals.

India and the United States: Account for 7% and 5%, respectively, of imports, with refined petroleum being a key import from India.

In 2023, imports totalled $123.541 billion, resulting in a trade balance near equilibrium but exposing vulnerabilities in energy and industrial inputs.

Foreign Exchange Reserves

South Africa's foreign exchange and gold reserves, valued at $62.492 billion in 2023, provide a buffer against external shocks and currency volatility. These reserves are critical for maintaining investor confidence, funding critical imports, and stabilizing the rand in the face of global economic uncertainty.

Infrastructure and Connectivity

Infrastructure is a critical pillar of South Africa's economic growth and regional influence, supporting its trade and industrial sectors.

Transportation: A Regional Hub

South Africa boasts an extensive transportation network that underpins its role as a regional logistics hub:

Roadways: With over 750,000 kilometers of roadways, including 158,124 kilometers of paved roads, the country has one of the most extensive road networks in Africa, facilitating domestic and regional trade.

Railways: The country's 30,400-kilometer railway network, primarily narrow gauge, is vital for moving goods, particularly minerals, to ports for export. Efforts to modernize this network are ongoing to improve efficiency and reduce costs.

Ports: Major ports, including Durban, Cape Town, Richards Bay, and Port Elizabeth, are pivotal for international trade. Durban is one of Africa's busiest ports, handling containerized goods, while Richards Bay specializes in bulk commodities like coal.

Energy Challenges: Addressing a Crisis

Energy infrastructure represents one of South Africa's most pressing challenges:

Electricity Supply: Chronic shortages and load-shedding due to mismanagement at Eskom have hindered industrial production, increased business costs, and deterred foreign investment.

Coal Dependency: Coal remains the dominant energy source, accounting for 87.8% of electricity generation in 2022, despite its environmental impact.

Renewable Energy: Wind and solar energy represented just 6.9% of total installed capacity in 2022, signaling the urgent need for accelerated investments in renewable energy sources.

Nuclear Energy: South Africa operates two nuclear reactors, contributing 4.4% of electricity generation with a combined capacity of 1.85 GW.

Connectivity: Expanding Digital Infrastructure

South Africa's telecommunications infrastructure is among the most advanced in Africa:

Mobile Connectivity: The country had 100.26 million mobile subscriptions in 2022, a penetration rate of 167 subscriptions per 100 inhabitants.

Broadband Access: Fixed broadband remains limited, with only 1.31 million subscriptions in 2022, but investments in fiber-optic networks aim to expand coverage, especially in underserved rural areas.

International Links: South Africa is connected to global digital networks through submarine fiber-optic cables, enabling efficient data transmission and supporting its growing tech sector.

Enhancing infrastructure and addressing energy challenges are critical for South Africa's future. Investment in renewable energy, modernizing transportation networks, and expanding digital connectivity can drive sustainable growth, reduce inequalities, and solidify South Africa's position as a key player in global trade and investment.

Investment Opportunities: Sectors Poised for Growth

South Africa presents a dynamic investment landscape, leveraging its rich resource base, industrial potential, and evolving policy frameworks to attract both domestic and foreign capital. Several sectors stand out for their growth potential, offering significant opportunities for investors.

Mining and Resources: A Global Leader

South Africa's mining sector is a vital component of its economy and continues to offer robust investment opportunities:

Critical Minerals: The country's position as the largest global producer of platinum and a leading supplier of chromium and gold makes it a cornerstone for investors in mining and metallurgy. Demand for rare earth elements and vanadium, driven by green technologies, further underscores the sector's relevance.

Exploration and Technology: Investments in advanced mining technologies, including automation and sustainable extraction methods, can enhance efficiency and environmental compliance.

Export Markets: South Africa's established trade links with major economies such as China, Germany, and India provide a ready market for its mineral exports, ensuring consistent demand.

Renewable Energy: A Green Transition

South Africa's energy sector is undergoing a significant transformation, creating a wealth of opportunities for renewable energy investments:

Policy Support: The government's Integrated Resource Plan emphasizes the diversification of the energy mix, targeting an increased share for wind, solar, and other renewable sources.

Solar and Wind Projects: With its favorable climate and vast open spaces, South Africa is well-suited for large-scale solar farms and wind projects. Recent auctions under the Renewable Energy Independent Power Producer Procurement Programme (REIPPPP) have already attracted global interest.

Grid Modernization: Investments in modernizing the energy grid to accommodate decentralized renewable generation and storage solutions are critical to overcoming energy distribution challenges.

Agribusiness: Unlocking Potential

Agriculture, while contributing a modest portion to GDP, holds untapped potential for growth and export:

Diversified Output: South Africa is a significant producer of crops such as sugarcane, maize, and fruits like grapes and citrus. Expanding export markets, particularly in Europe and Asia, offers significant growth opportunities.

Value-Added Processing: Investments in agro-processing industries, including food and beverage manufacturing, can enhance the value chain and create jobs in rural areas.

Technological Integration: Precision agriculture, irrigation systems, and advanced farming techniques represent areas where technology can boost productivity and sustainability.

Technology: A Thriving Digital Market

South Africa's technology sector, bolstered by its advanced telecommunications infrastructure, is a beacon for innovation and growth:

Telecom and Broadband: As Africa's most developed telecom market, South Africa offers opportunities in expanding fiber-optic networks and mobile broadband services. With mobile penetration exceeding 167 subscriptions per 100 inhabitants, the demand for faster and more reliable internet is growing.

Digital Services: The rapid adoption of e-commerce, fintech, and online education platforms underscores the potential for digital transformation investments.

Data Centers and Cloud Services: With increasing digitization, there is a growing need for data center infrastructure and cloud computing services, providing lucrative opportunities for global tech firms.

Infrastructure Development: Building the Future

South Africa's infrastructure development agenda provides a range of investment opportunities:

Transportation: Modernizing and expanding the railway and port systems to enhance trade logistics is a high priority. Key projects in major ports like Durban and Cape Town aim to increase capacity and efficiency.

Urban Development: Investments in housing, urban planning, and smart city technologies can address challenges posed by rapid urbanization.

Water Management: Infrastructure for water conservation and distribution, including desalination and recycling systems, is increasingly critical to counteract droughts and rising demand.

Manufacturing: Revitalizing Industry

South Africa's industrial base offers potential for growth in key manufacturing subsectors:

Automotive Industry: As a regional hub for automobile production and exports, investments in electric vehicle (EV) production and supporting infrastructure could position South Africa as a leader in the African EV market.

Pharmaceuticals and Chemicals: Expanding local production of pharmaceuticals and specialty chemicals can reduce reliance on imports and support regional healthcare needs.

South Africa's investment landscape is marked by its resource wealth, policy-driven energy transition, and thriving tech sector. By aligning with government priorities, such as renewable energy adoption and infrastructure modernization, and leveraging untapped potential in agribusiness and technology, investors can capitalize on the country's dynamic growth trajectory. A long-term perspective, combined with strategic risk management, is essential to navigating this diverse and promising market.

Navigating Risks

While South Africa offers compelling opportunities for investors, it also presents a complex risk landscape that requires careful assessment and strategic planning. These risks are shaped by its political environment, socioeconomic challenges, and infrastructure inefficiencies.

Political Landscape: Governance and Reform

South Africa's political stability is notable in the African context, but underlying issues can affect investor confidence:

Corruption and Governance: Despite ongoing efforts under President Cyril Ramaphosa's administration to combat corruption, instances of mismanagement within key institutions, including state-owned enterprises like Eskom, remain a concern.

Policy Uncertainty: Inconsistent implementation of economic and regulatory reforms, such as those related to land redistribution and labor laws, creates unpredictability that can deter long-term investments.

International Relations: South Africa's role within BRICS (Brazil, Russia, India, China, South Africa) and its alignment with global powers affect trade dynamics and diplomatic relations, adding a layer of complexity to external risk considerations.

Economic Inequality: Social and Fiscal Pressures

Deep-seated economic inequality continues to pose challenges for sustained growth and stability:

Urban-Rural Divide: Significant disparities between urban hubs and rural regions exacerbate poverty and limit the broad-based benefits of economic development.

Public Protests: High unemployment, particularly among the youth, has fueled public dissatisfaction, sometimes manifesting as protests and disruptions that can impact business operations.

Fiscal Pressures: High public debt, which stood at 76.55% of GDP in 2022, and limited fiscal space constrain the government's ability to address inequality through infrastructure projects and social programs.

Utility Reliability: Energy and Infrastructure Struggles

South Africa's infrastructure, while extensive, faces challenges that impede economic productivity:

Power Outages: Persistent load-shedding due to inefficiencies at Eskom impacts industries, services, and daily life. In 2022, transmission and distribution losses reached 25.285 billion kWh, underlining the scale of inefficiency.

Aging Infrastructure: Delayed investments in modernization across energy, water, and transport networks create bottlenecks that slow economic activity and increase operational costs for businesses.

Water Scarcity: Limited renewable water resources (51.35 billion cubic meters in 2020) and growing demand place pressure on agricultural and industrial sectors, particularly during periods of prolonged drought.

Labor Market Challenges: Strikes and Productivity

South Africa's labor market dynamics present additional risks:

Frequent Strikes: Labor disputes, particularly in mining and public services, disrupt operations and can lead to significant financial losses.

Productivity Gaps: Skills mismatches and underinvestment in workforce development hinder industrial competitiveness and innovation.

Environmental Risks: Sustainability and Climate Change

Environmental factors add a layer of risk for long-term investments:

Climate Vulnerability: Prolonged droughts and extreme weather events threaten agriculture, water supply, and infrastructure resilience.

Regulatory Pressures: As global markets shift toward sustainability, South Africa's heavy reliance on coal-based energy (87.8% of capacity in 2022) may face increasing scrutiny and pressure to decarbonize.

Financial Risks: Exchange Rates and Debt

South Africa's financial landscape is not immune to external shocks:

Currency Volatility: Fluctuations in the rand, influenced by global commodity prices and investor sentiment, can impact profit margins and cost structures for international businesses.

External Debt: The country's external debt of $53.43 billion in 2022 poses repayment risks, particularly in the context of rising global interest rates.

Strategic Risk Management

Investors must adopt a proactive approach to mitigating risks in South Africa by:

Policy Engagement: Close collaboration with local stakeholders and monitoring of regulatory changes can help anticipate and adapt to policy shifts.

Infrastructure Partnerships: Partnering in infrastructure modernization projects can minimize operational disruptions while contributing to long-term economic stability.

ESG Integration: Emphasizing environmental, social, and governance (ESG) principles in investment strategies can align with global trends and mitigate reputational risks.

Diversification: Investing across multiple sectors and geographies within South Africa can reduce exposure to localized disruptions or sector-specific challenges.

By carefully navigating these risks, investors can unlock South Africa's potential while contributing to its broader economic and social development.

Chapter Conclusion: Vision for the Future

South Africa's path forward hinges on strategic reforms and sustainable development. With its resource wealth and industrial base, the country holds vast potential for investors who can align with its developmental priorities and manage the inherent risks. By addressing its structural challenges, South Africa can position itself as a gateway to African markets and a key player on the global stage.

Chapter (7)

Iran: Balancing Rich Resources and Challenging Reforms

'BRICS is a symbol of such a change in global relations that can help solve the problems of the world community"

President Ebrahim Raisi

Iran stands at the crossroads of ancient heritage and contemporary global dynamics. Rich in natural resources and strategically located, the country presents a tapestry of opportunities and challenges shaped by its economic, investment, and regulatory landscape. Despite international sanctions and internal pressures, Iran's economic trajectory reveals resilience and potential for transformative growth.

A Nation of Strategic Importance

Spanning 1.65 million square kilometers, Iran boasts a unique position connecting the Middle East, Central Asia, and South Asia. With a population of 88.4 million, predominantly urbanized (77%), cities like Tehran, Mashhad, and Esfahan are hubs of economic and cultural activity. Iran's educated workforce and youthful demographic profile, with a median age of 33.8 years, provide a foundation for innovation and development.

Economic Resilience Amid Complex Dynamics

Iran's economy reflects a blend of state control, resource wealth, and reform aspirations.

GDP and Growth: The nominal GDP of $401.5 billion (2023) and a purchasing power parity (PPP) GDP of $1.44 trillion rank Iran 22nd globally. Despite high inflation and sanctions, Iran managed a 4.95% GDP growth in 2023, driven by industrial expansion and modest consumer confidence recovery.

Inflation and Employment: Inflation remains a critical challenge, reaching 44.58% in 2023 due to currency devaluation and economic sanctions. Unemployment is 9.1%, with youth unemployment at 22.8%, emphasizing the need for targeted labor market reforms.

Sectoral Contributions: The economy is heavily influenced by industry (41.8% of GDP) and services (42.7%), while agriculture contributes 13%. Industrial production grew by 8.84% in 2023, reflecting the resilience of key sectors.

Energy and Trade: Pillars of Stability

Iran's economy is deeply rooted in its abundant energy resources and strategically important trade relationships. Together, these sectors form the backbone of the nation's economic resilience and growth potential, even amid challenging global dynamics and persistent sanctions.

Energy Resources

Iran is a global energy powerhouse, boasting some of the largest reserves of fossil fuels in the world:

- **Natural Gas:** Iran holds the world's second-largest proven natural gas reserves at 34 trillion cubic meters, making it a key player in global energy markets. Its production in 2022 reached 263.28 billion cubic meters, with 19.25 billion cubic meters exported. While the majority of its exports target regional partners like Turkey and Iraq, the potential for broader international partnerships remains untapped due to sanctions.

- **Crude Oil:** Iran's crude oil reserves, the fourth-largest globally, are estimated at 208.6 billion barrels. Daily production in 2023 reached approximately 3.985 million barrels, with significant volumes allocated for domestic use and export.

- **Refined Petroleum and Gasoline:** Iran's refining capacity supports its energy independence, though increasing domestic consumption strains export potential.

Energy Infrastructure: Fossil fuels dominate Iran's energy mix, contributing 93.5% of its electricity generation.

Hydroelectric power (4.4%) and nuclear energy (1.7%) represent early efforts to diversify, while renewable sources like solar and wind contribute minimally but are poised for future expansion. These efforts are supported by substantial investments in nuclear technology, such as the operational Bushehr nuclear power plant and a second reactor under construction.

Challenges and Opportunities in Energy: Despite its wealth of resources, Iran faces challenges in modernizing its aging infrastructure, improving efficiency, and accessing global markets. Strategic partnerships with China and Russia have provided some relief, enabling technological and financial cooperation, particularly in energy projects. However, sanctions have restricted access to advanced equipment and international financing, limiting Iran's ability to fully exploit its reserves.

Trade Dynamics

Iran's trade activities are crucial for its economic stability, balancing robust exports with strategic imports:

Exports

Iran's exports totalled $110.88 billion in 2022, underscoring its reliance on energy products. Key export commodities include:

Natural Gas and Oil Derivatives: A significant portion of export revenue stems from energy, including crude oil, ethylene polymers, and refined copper.

Petrochemicals: Iran's growing petrochemical sector supports diversification within energy-based exports.

Agricultural Products: Wheat, vegetables, and other agricultural goods contribute to export diversity, albeit on a smaller scale.

Trade Partners

China is Iran's largest trading partner, accounting for 36% of exports and 28% of imports in 2022. Turkey (20% of exports) and India (4%) are other significant export destinations, reflecting Iran's efforts to deepen regional ties. Imports primarily originate from China and the UAE (19%), highlighting their roles as crucial suppliers of machinery, electronics, and vehicle parts.

Imports

Iran's imports, valued at $102.47 billion in 2022, focus on essential commodities and technology:

Machinery and Technology: Broadcasting equipment, vehicle parts, and industrial tools support domestic manufacturing and infrastructure development.

Agricultural Products: Corn, soybeans, and rice are essential imports, ensuring food security.

Strategic Position and Trade Corridors

Iran's geographic location at the crossroads of the Middle East, Central Asia, and South Asia enhances its importance as a trade hub. Key elements include:

Strategic Ports: Facilities like Bandar Abbas on the Persian Gulf enable efficient export and import operations, while the development of the Chabahar Port in collaboration with India provides access to South Asian markets and bypasses regional bottlenecks.

Pipeline Networks: Iran's extensive network includes 20,794 km of natural gas pipelines and 8,625 km of oil pipelines, facilitating energy exports to regional partners.

Future Directions in Energy and Trade

To enhance the sustainability and resilience of its energy and trade sectors, Iran is pursuing several initiatives:

Diversification: Expanding renewable energy capacity and developing value-added petrochemical products to reduce reliance on crude oil exports.

Technological Advancement: Modernizing its energy infrastructure with the help of domestic innovations and partnerships with non-Western allies like Russia and China.

Regional Integration: Strengthening economic ties with neighboring countries through free trade agreements and collaborative infrastructure projects.

Sanction Resilience: Developing barter-based trade and leveraging alternative payment systems to mitigate the impact of financial restrictions.

Demographics and Workforce

Iran's demographic structure offers growth potential but necessitates strategic planning:

Labor Force: With 29.2 million workers, the economy benefits from a relatively educated population (88.7% literacy rate) and 15 years of schooling expectancy. However, addressing unemployment and underemployment is vital for economic stability.

Urbanization and Population Trends: Urban growth (1.32% annual rate) aligns with broader economic modernization. However, rural areas face slower development, highlighting the need for inclusive policies.

Regulatory Reforms

Iran's regulatory environment continues to evolve, aiming to address systemic inefficiencies, attract foreign investment, and enhance economic stability. While challenges persist, several focused efforts reflect Iran's drive toward modernization and resilience.

Financial Sector and Banking Reforms

The financial sector in Iran is undergoing incremental reforms to align with international standards and attract capital:

Banking Transparency: Efforts to combat money laundering and comply with global financial norms are underway, although progress is hindered by limited international engagement due to sanctions.

Central Bank Policies: The Central Bank of Iran is focused on stabilizing the currency and controlling inflation through stricter monetary policies and improved financial oversight.

Trade and Export Regulations

Iran has implemented measures to streamline export processes and reduce bureaucratic bottlenecks:

Customs Reforms: Digitizing customs procedures has improved efficiency, making cross-border trade faster and more predictable.

Export Incentives: Policies aimed at encouraging non-oil exports, including reduced tariffs and subsidies for exporters in agriculture and petrochemicals, have shown modest success.

Legal and Business Framework

Creating a more business-friendly environment remains a priority:

Ease of Doing Business: Simplifying business registration and licensing processes has been a focus to encourage small and medium-sized enterprises (SMEs).

Intellectual Property Protections: Iran is enhancing intellectual property laws to attract technology firms and foster innovation, particularly in its growing startup ecosystem.

Investment Landscape

Iran's investment potential spans multiple sectors, leveraging its rich resources, strategic location, and youthful workforce. Despite sanctions, domestic and regional investors are exploring opportunities in key areas.

Mining and Natural Resources

Iran's vast reserves of minerals, including copper, zinc, and iron ore, present lucrative opportunities:

Mining Potential: The underexplored mining sector is ripe for investment, particularly in extraction and processing facilities.

Value-Added Products: Encouraging the production of finished goods from raw materials could boost export revenues and reduce dependency on volatile energy markets.

Tourism and Cultural Heritage

Tourism, a sector with untapped potential, is gaining attention:

Cultural and Historical Assets: Iran's 28 UNESCO World Heritage Sites and rich cultural history attract international interest, offering opportunities in eco-tourism, cultural tours, and hospitality.

Religious Tourism: Pilgrimage sites like Mashhad and Qom hold significant potential for growth, supported by improved infrastructure and services.

Renewable Energy Expansion

Iran's commitment to diversifying its energy portfolio opens new avenues:

Solar and Wind Energy: Favorable geographic and climatic conditions make Iran an attractive destination for solar and wind power projects.

Hydropower Development: Opportunities exist to expand Iran's hydroelectric capacity beyond its current 4.4% contribution to the energy mix.

Logistics and Trade Corridors

Iran's role as a trade hub offers investment prospects in logistics and transportation:

Railway Expansion: Enhancing the 8,483 km railway network to improve connectivity with regional trade partners, including projects linked to the International North-South Transport Corridor.

Port Upgrades: Investments in modernizing ports like Bandar Abbas and Chabahar could increase Iran's competitiveness in global trade.

Healthcare and Pharmaceuticals

The healthcare sector is an emerging field for investment:

Medical Tourism: Competitive pricing and skilled healthcare professionals attract patients from neighboring countries.

Pharmaceuticals: Iran's robust domestic production base offers potential for partnerships in research, development, and exports.

Information and Communication Technology (ICT)

Iran's youthful and tech-savvy population drives demand in the ICT sector:

AI and Data Analytics: Investments in artificial intelligence applications for agriculture, healthcare, and urban planning are gaining traction.

E-Governance Solutions: Modernizing government services through technology

Challenges and Pathways Forward

Iran's economic landscape is marked by significant challenges that require strategic interventions, balanced by emerging opportunities that highlight the country's potential for growth and reform.

Sanctions and Isolation

International sanctions have been a persistent impediment to Iran's economic integration and global market access. Sanctions targeting Iran's energy exports, financial institutions, and critical sectors have curtailed foreign direct investment (FDI) and limited technological advancements.

The country's response includes deepening ties with nations like China and Russia to counterbalance Western isolation. China, Iran's largest trading partner, accounts for 36% of its exports and 28% of its imports. Strategic agreements, such as the 25-year cooperation deal with China, reflect Iran's pivot towards Eastern alliances. Similarly, Russia's partnership with Iran extends to energy, defense, and trade, though these partnerships provide only partial relief from the broader economic stagnation caused by sanctions. While such collaborations offer lifelines, they inherently limit Iran's diversification of economic ties and reinforce dependency on a narrow set of partners.

Pathways forward may include diplomatic efforts to revive the Joint Comprehensive Plan of Action (JCPOA) or develop new multilateral agreements to ease restrictions, fostering a broader reintegration into the global economy.

Inflation and Currency Stability

Inflation, at a staggering 44.58% in 2023, reflects systemic weaknesses in fiscal management exacerbated by sanctions. Currency devaluation and limited access to foreign exchange reserves have destabilized the Iranian rial, maintaining an official exchange rate of 42,000 rials per USD since 2019. Addressing inflation requires comprehensive monetary reforms, including:

Exchange Rate Liberalization: Introducing a market-driven exchange rate to reflect true economic conditions.

Diversification of Revenue Streams: Reducing overreliance on oil exports by promoting industrialization and non-oil sectors.

Fiscal Discipline: Streamlining subsidies and addressing inefficiencies in public spending to curb inflationary pressures.

Such measures could stabilize the rial and restore domestic and foreign investor confidence, although they would need to be carefully managed to minimize social upheaval.

Social and Labor Dynamics

Iran's youthful and educated workforce is a critical asset, yet unemployment, particularly among the youth (22.8%) and women (35.5%), poses significant challenges. The workforce participation rate for women remains one of the lowest in the region, limiting the country's economic potential. Gender disparities are entrenched by sociocultural norms and insufficient legal protections, which restrict women's access to certain professions and leadership roles.

To address these dynamics, Iran could implement:

Labor Market Reforms: Encourage entrepreneurship and create job opportunities in technology and service sectors to absorb unemployed youth.

Gender Inclusion Policies: Develop initiatives to promote women's workforce participation through education, vocational training, and legal reforms ensuring workplace equality.

Social Safety Nets: Expand welfare programs to support vulnerable groups and mitigate the impact of economic restructuring.

Inclusive growth strategies are essential not only for economic stability but also for fostering social cohesion and reducing inequality.

Structural Reforms and Governance

The Iranian economy's state-controlled structure and regulatory inefficiencies impede private sector development. Bureaucratic hurdles, corruption, and limited transparency deter both domestic and foreign investors. Efforts to reform state-owned enterprises (SOEs), streamline regulatory processes, and promote accountability are critical to fostering a more dynamic economic environment. Pathways include:

Privatization Initiatives: Encourage private sector participation by reducing the dominance of SOEs in key sectors.

Digitalization of Governance: Implement e-governance tools to reduce red tape and enhance transparency in business operations.

Anti-Corruption Measures: Strengthen legal frameworks to combat corruption and improve investor trust.

Environmental Challenges

Iran faces significant environmental issues, including water scarcity, air pollution, and land degradation. Over-reliance on water-intensive agriculture and inefficient resource management exacerbate these problems. Mitigation strategies include:

Sustainable Agriculture Practices: Introduce water-efficient irrigation systems and crop diversification.

Renewable Energy Investments: Expand solar, wind, and hydroelectric capacities to reduce reliance on fossil fuels and mitigate air pollution.

Climate Adaptation Programs: Enhance resilience to droughts and floods through infrastructure development and policy interventions.

Iran's path forward demands bold reforms that address systemic economic vulnerabilities while leveraging its inherent strengths. Strategic diplomacy to reduce sanctions, comprehensive monetary reforms, and inclusive social policies could unlock Iran's potential for sustained growth. Additionally, fostering transparency, environmental sustainability, and innovation will be critical in transforming challenges into opportunities, ensuring long-term prosperity.

.

Chapter Conclusion: A Future of Transformation

Iran's economic narrative is one of untapped potential amidst significant challenges. By leveraging its resource wealth and youthful workforce while pursuing regulatory reforms, Iran can chart a path toward sustainable development. For investors willing to navigate its complexities, opportunities abound in energy, technology, and infrastructure. With the right strategies, Iran's resilience and reform efforts can pave the way for enduring prosperity.

Chapter (8)

Egypt Navigating Economic Transformation: Challenges, Opportunities, and a Glimpse of Hope

"Raise the voice of the Global South with regard to the various issues and development challenges"

President Abdel Fattah El-Sisi

Egypt, situated in Northern Africa and bridging the continents of Africa and Asia through the Sinai Peninsula, occupies a strategic geographic location. Bordered by the Mediterranean Sea to the north, the Red Sea to the east, Libya to the west, and Sudan to the south, Egypt also serves as a critical transit hub due to the Suez Canal, connecting the Indian Ocean and Mediterranean Sea. Covering over 1 million square kilometers, the vast majority of its population of approximately 111 million people is concentrated within a narrow strip along the fertile Nile River and its delta, which constitutes only about 5% of the country's land area. The remainder is dominated by arid deserts. This demographic concentration has implications for urban development, resource allocation, and economic planning.

Historically, the nation's economy has been shaped by its control of critical trade routes and natural resources, including petroleum, natural gas, and phosphates. Recent reports by the IMF and other global organizations highlight Egypt's ambitious economic reform agenda, which includes bolstering the private sector, unifying its foreign exchange rate, and enhancing public fiscal discipline. Challenges persist, including high inflation and external vulnerabilities exacerbated by regional instability. Nonetheless, investments such as the $35 billion Ras El-Hekma development project on the Mediterranean coast, alongside ongoing structural reforms, signal emerging opportunities for investors. With a young population—nearly 34% under 14 years—and increasing urbanization, Egypt's demographic trends further underscore its potential as a dynamic market in the Arab world and beyond.

Battling Headwinds, Seeking Stability

Egypt's recent economic performance has been marked by significant challenges, with growth slowing to 3.0% in FY2023/24, as reported by the IMF. The real GDP (purchasing power parity) was estimated at $1.912 trillion moving up from $1.842 trillion in 2022 and $1.729 trillion in 2021 using 2021 dollars, while the GDP using official exchange rate was estimated at $396.002 billion in 2023.

51.3% of the GDP in 2023 was produced by services, 32.1% by industry and 11.6% by agriculture. This deceleration stems from a confluence of external and domestic factors that have constrained economic activity:

Global Economic Slowdown

The global economic environment has been fraught with uncertainty, largely influenced by the ongoing conflict in Ukraine, persistently high inflation in major economies, and the resulting tightening of global financial conditions. These dynamics have impacted Egypt in several ways:

- **Tourism Revenues:** Declined significantly due to reduced global mobility and the lingering effects of geopolitical tensions.
- **Exports:** Weakened global demand has suppressed Egypt's export performance, compounding its trade balance pressures.
- **Foreign Direct Investment (FDI):** Net FDI inflows dropped to an estimated 2.5% of GDP in FY2023/24 from 9.3% the previous year, reflecting global risk aversion and domestic constraints.

Regional Conflicts

Egypt has borne the economic brunt of instability in its region, particularly the Gaza-Israel conflict. Key impacts include:

- **Suez Canal Revenues**: Disruptions in the Red Sea reduced receipts by almost 50% year-on-year in early 2024, costing approximately $375 million in January alone.

- **Tourism Sector**: Further pressure on a critical industry, already strained by global trends, as tourists shy away from the region amid heightened security concerns. These disruptions have compounded Egypt's foreign exchange shortages and fiscal pressures.

Domestic Challenges

High Inflation: Inflation surged to **38% in September 2023**, driven by exchange rate volatility, constrained imports, and rising input costs. While inflation declined to **27.5% by June 2024** due to aggressive monetary tightening, it continues to erode purchasing power, strain household budgets, and heighten uncertainty for businesses.

Borrowing Costs: In response to inflation, the Central Bank of Egypt (CBE) raised policy rates to **27.75%**, creating high nominal borrowing costs. This has constrained private-sector investment and dampened consumer spending, slowing overall economic activity.

Debt Levels: General government debt stands at **96.4% of GDP in FY2023/24**, a level exacerbated by the cumulative effects of past deficits, exchange rate depreciation, and rising interest payments. Debt-servicing costs absorb a significant portion of fiscal resources, limiting public spending on growth-enhancing projects.

Poverty and Income Inequality: Approximately **29.7% of Egypt's population lives below the national poverty line** (2019 CIA The World Factbook Estimate). Poverty remains a persistent challenge, particularly in rural and southern regions where income disparities are more pronounced. The Gini Index, which measures income inequality, was **31.9** in 2019, indicating moderate inequality levels.

Gendered Unemployment: Youth unemployment remains a critical issue, with the overall rate for ages 15-24 standing at **19% in 2023**. The disparity between genders is stark:

- Male youth unemployment: 12.6%
- Female youth unemployment: 49.2%

These figures underscore structural barriers to female labor force participation and the broader need for gender-inclusive economic policies

Signs of Stabilization and Reform Progress

Despite these headwinds, there are notable positive developments that suggest Egypt is laying the groundwork for stabilization and recovery:

Commitment to Reform Program: Egypt's government has taken decisive steps to implement the economic reform program under the IMF's Extended Fund Facility. This program aims to restore macroeconomic stability and foster private-sector-led growth. Key reforms include:

- Divesting state-owned assets to reduce public sector dominance.

- Strengthening public investment management to control expenditure.

Exchange Rate Unification: The unification of the exchange rate in March 2024 eliminated a significant parallel market premium and restored confidence in the foreign exchange market. This move:

- Alleviated foreign currency shortages, clearing backlogs of $7–8 billion.
- Enhanced business access to foreign currency, critical for import-dependent industries.
- Helped stabilize the Egyptian pound and improved prospects for external financing.

Monetary Policy Tightening: To combat inflation, the CBE implemented aggressive rate hikes totalling 800 basis points in early 2024. While contractionary in the short term, these measures have:

- Anchored inflation expectations, setting the stage for medium-term price stability.
- Strengthened the credibility of monetary policy, a critical component of macroeconomic management.

Investor Confidence: A combination of reforms and stabilization measures has contributed to increased demand for Egyptian pound-denominated assets, including Treasury securities. This is evidenced by:

- Narrower sovereign bond spreads, with a 300-basis point tightening following the announcement of the $35 billion Ras El-Hekma investment deal.
- Improved capital market conditions, driven by reduced exchange rate volatility and structural reforms.

While Egypt's challenges remain significant, these recent developments offer hope for a more stable economic trajectory. Sustained reform implementation, disciplined fiscal and monetary management, and efforts to reduce the state's footprint in the economy will be critical to maintaining momentum. With these measures, Egypt aims to restore macroeconomic stability and create a more conducive environment for private investment, setting the stage for long-term sustainable growth.

Fiscal Consolidation: A Balancing Act

Egypt is grappling with a complex fiscal landscape characterized by high public debt, substantial financing needs, and the imperative to protect its most vulnerable populations. The government's gross debt is projected to reach **96.4% of GDP in FY2024/25**, reflecting the accumulated effects of past deficits, exchange rate depreciation, and rising interest costs. This high debt burden not only limits fiscal space but also heightens Egypt's vulnerability to economic and external shocks.

To navigate these challenges, the government has embarked on a strategy of fiscal consolidation aimed at reducing the debt-to-GDP ratio while safeguarding essential social expenditures. Central to this strategy is the target of achieving a primary surplus of 3.5% of GDP (excluding divestment proceeds) in FY2024/25, a notable increase from the projected 2.5% primary surplus in FY2023/24. Achieving this ambitious target requires a multifaceted approach to balance growth, fiscal sustainability, and social protection.

Debt Reduction

Achieving the primary surplus target is essential to stabilizing and eventually reducing Egypt's debt-to-GDP ratio, which, after peaking in FY2023/24, is projected to follow a downward trajectory. This will be driven by:

Revenue Mobilization: The government plans to increase tax revenues by at least 3 percentage points of GDP by FY2026/27, through reforms such as:

- **VAT Amendments**: Simplifying the VAT system, reducing exemptions, and improving its efficiency and progressivity. The planned reforms are expected to contribute an additional 1% of GDP annually starting in FY2024/25.

- **Income Tax Law Overhaul**: This reform will improve the efficiency of tax collection, supported by new policies like carbon taxes and withholding taxes on freezone sales.
- **Strengthened Tax Administration**: Initiatives to broaden the tax base, combat evasion, and enhance enforcement mechanisms.

Expenditure Restraint: Public expenditure is projected to grow at a slower pace, with a focus on efficiency. The government aims to align fuel prices with cost-recovery levels by December 2025, freeing resources to reduce fiscal risks and redirect funds to targeted social programs.

Divestment Proceeds: Proceeds from privatization and asset sales, projected at 1% of GDP annually from FY2024/25 onward, will complement revenue generation efforts, reduce the debt burden, and fund critical social programs.

Safeguarding Essential Social Spending

Recognizing the critical role of social protection, the government is committed to maintaining and enhancing key programs, including:

- **Takaful and Karama**: Expanding these conditional cash transfer programs to provide safety nets for the most vulnerable.
- **Food Subsidies and Health Insurance**: These programs continue to serve as essential

components of Egypt's social protection framework.

- **New Social Initiatives**: The government has earmarked an additional **EGP 180 billion** for FY2024/25 to expand support for low-income households, mitigating the impact of subsidy reforms and inflation.

However, fiscal constraints limit the scope for introducing new initiatives or significantly scaling up existing programs, necessitating innovative approaches to balance fiscal discipline and social welfare.

Active Debt Management

The government is implementing a robust debt management strategy to reduce financing costs and mitigate rollover risks:

- **Lengthening Debt Maturity**: By extending the maturity of domestic debt through auctions, Egypt is reducing its exposure to short-term interest rate fluctuations and rollover risks.
- **Debt Swaps**: Agreements with pension and insurance funds to extend maturities on existing debt are being explored as a way to ease near-term financing pressures.
- **Transparent Public Investment**: A newly established framework ensures that public investment aligns with macroeconomic objectives

and avoids unsustainable off-budget borrowing. This includes better oversight of State-Owned Enterprises (SOEs) and their investments.

Key Success Factors

Several factors will determine the success of Egypt's fiscal consolidation strategy:

Sustained Reform Implementation: Consistent and transparent execution of revenue-enhancing measures, subsidy reforms, and fiscal management practices is critical to achieving the targeted surplus.

Economic Growth: While fiscal consolidation may dampen growth in the short term, the government projects a recovery to 4.5% growth in FY2024/25 and 5.5% by FY2026/27, supported by structural reforms and a more stable macroeconomic environment.

Social Stability: Maintaining public support for reforms is essential, particularly amid rising inflation and subsidy reductions. Enhanced communication about the long-term benefits of reforms and measures to protect vulnerable populations will be vital.

External Environment: Stable global commodity prices and improved investor sentiment will bolster fiscal and economic stability. Recent successes, such as the $35 billion Ras El-Hekma investment deal, demonstrate the potential for significant foreign inflows to support Egypt's fiscal goals.

Egypt's fiscal consolidation strategy represents a challenging yet essential endeavor to secure macroeconomic stability, reduce debt vulnerabilities, and create a sustainable fiscal position. While the government's commitment to reform is commendable, sustained efforts, careful management of risks, and strong public communication will be crucial for success. The strategy's ultimate test lies in its ability to balance debt reduction with the imperatives of growth and social protection, paving the way for a more inclusive and resilient economic future.

Structural Reforms: Paving the Path to Sustainable Growth

Macroeconomic stabilization is a crucial first step for Egypt, but its long-term economic success depends on the implementation of ambitious structural reforms. These reforms are essential to address deep-rooted challenges that have hindered private sector development, stifled productivity growth, and constrained Egypt's economic potential. To unlock these opportunities, Egypt's reform agenda focuses on redefining the role of the state, improving the business environment, and fostering a resilient financial sector.

Redefining the Role of the State

The State Ownership Policy represents a transformative step toward reducing the government's economic footprint and empowering the private sector. This policy aims to foster a competitive market environment by levelling the playing field between state-owned enterprises (SOEs) and private businesses. Key elements include:

Divestment of State-Owned Assets:

- The government plans to generate **$3.6 billion in dollar inflows** from divestment in FY2024/25. Recent divestments, such as the **Eastern Tobacco Company** and **Gabal El Zeit Wind Farm**, highlight progress, with assets being sold to both domestic and foreign investors.
- Proceeds from these divestments are earmarked for debt reduction, freeing up fiscal resources while attracting private-sector expertise and investment into non-strategic sectors.

Strengthening Corporate Governance:

- To improve the efficiency and performance of SOEs, the government is creating a central unit within the Prime Minister's office to oversee SOE governance and facilitate divestment.
- This includes new legislation aimed at increasing accountability and operational transparency, ensuring SOEs align with global governance standards.

Enhancing Transparency:

- Expanding the SOE database and publishing annual aggregate financial reports are steps toward improved visibility and fair competition.
- The government is committed to requiring SOEs to adopt international financial reporting standards (IFRS) and disclose procurement activities to prevent favoritism and improve investor confidence.

Creating a More Conducive Business Environment

Improving the business environment is pivotal to unlocking private-sector growth and attracting foreign direct investment. To achieve this, the government is prioritizing the following:

Streamlining Regulations:

- Egypt's regulatory framework has long been a bottleneck for businesses. The government is working on reducing administrative burdens, fast-tracking business registrations, and improving licensing processes.
- The "Golden License" system for strategic projects, which simplifies approval processes, is a cornerstone of these efforts, particularly for renewable energy and logistics investments.

Enhancing Trade Facilitation:

- Trade logistics improvements are critical for boosting exports and attracting investment. The introduction of a risk-based customs clearance system and the "Green Lane" initiative for low-risk cargo are expected to expedite processes significantly.
- As part of its trade facilitation agenda, Egypt has signed agreements to harmonize customs standards with key trading partners in Europe and Africa, leveraging its strategic geographic location.

Strengthening the Competition Framework:

- The government is advancing reforms to empower the Egyptian Competition Authority (ECA), including granting it enhanced enforcement powers and operational independence.
- These reforms aim to curb anti-competitive practices, foster innovation, and ensure small and medium enterprises (SMEs) have a fair opportunity to thrive.

Fostering a More Resilient and Competitive Financial Sector

A robust financial sector is fundamental to supporting economic growth and facilitating private investment. Key reforms include:

Enhancing Governance in State-Owned Banks:

- State-owned banks account for a significant portion of Egypt's financial system, but improving their governance practices is critical. The government is commissioning independent assessments of their policies, procedures, and risk controls.
- Additionally, the Ministry of Finance is exploring ways to separate public lending from commercial banking functions to ensure a more focused allocation of resources.

Promoting Competition:

Increasing competition in the banking sector is essential to improve access to finance for businesses and reduce borrowing costs. The government plans to incentivize private banks to expand operations and encourage the entry of new financial institutions.

Ensuring Financial Stability:

- Strengthened prudential regulations and closer monitoring of banks' exposure to public sector agencies are central to maintaining financial stability. As of late 2023, the Central Bank of Egypt (CBE) reported progress in reducing the foreign exchange liabilities of banks, ensuring a more stable currency environment.
- Risk management practices are being overhauled, particularly in the wake of exchange rate unification, to safeguard the banking system from future shocks.

Navigating a Complex Path

The IMF acknowledges that Egypt's structural reform agenda is both ambitious and challenging. Overcoming entrenched interests, addressing social sensitivities, and ensuring effective implementation require strong political will, consistent follow-through, and stakeholder buy-in.

Key challenges include:

- **Political Economy Risks**: Resistance from entrenched stakeholders in SOEs and regulatory bodies could delay reforms.
- **Social Impact**: The government must mitigate the social costs of reforms, particularly subsidy reductions, to maintain public support.
- **External Risks**: Regional instability, volatile commodity prices, and global economic headwinds could derail reform progress.

While the external and domestic risks to Egypt's economy remain significant, the government's commitment to its structural reform program offers a pathway to long-term growth. Measures such as exchange rate unification, SOE divestments, and trade facilitation are already yielding early results, evidenced by improved investor confidence and reduced foreign exchange backlogs.

If successfully executed, these reforms could pave the way for a more competitive, inclusive, and prosperous economy, enabling Egypt to unlock its vast economic potential. However, continued vigilance, adaptability, and robust policy coordination will be essential to ensure a durable recovery and sustainable growth.

Key Takeaways for Investors: Navigating Egypt's Evolving Landscape

As the country implements ambitious reforms to stabilize its economy and foster growth, a cautious and informed investment strategy is crucial. Below are expanded key takeaways for investors navigating Egypt's evolving landscape:

Thorough Risk Assessment is Paramount

Investors must account for Egypt's complex risk profile, which combines both significant opportunities and notable challenges

Acknowledge the Complex Risk Profile

Geopolitical Risks: Regional instability, particularly the ongoing Palestinian-Israel conflict and Red Sea disruptions, continues to affect trade, tourism, and investor sentiment. These challenges underscore the importance of assessing exposure to regional shocks when evaluating investment opportunities.

Inflationary Pressures: Although inflation eased to **27.5% in June 2024** from a peak of **38% in September 2023**, it remains high. Persistently elevated inflation erodes purchasing power and increases input costs for businesses, posing risks to profitability.

Fiscal Vulnerabilities: With gross public debt projected at **96.4% of GDP in FY2024/25**, coupled with large financing needs and contingent liabilities from SOEs, fiscal risks are substantial. These factors may influence government policies and affect investor returns, especially in sectors dependent on public contracts or subsidies.

Conduct Comprehensive Due Diligence:

Investors should thoroughly assess sector-specific risks and opportunities, taking into account external shocks, inflation, exchange rate volatility, and regulatory changes. For example, sectors such as renewable energy, logistics, and technology are aligned with national priorities and reform agendas, presenting lower-risk opportunities.

Evaluating macroeconomic scenarios is essential, particularly with respect to foreign exchange availability, as the unification of Egypt's exchange rate system has alleviated but not eliminated currency risks.

Prioritize Investments Aligned with Sustainable Growth

Egypt's reform agenda emphasizes private-sector-led growth and economic diversification, creating opportunities for investments that align with these objectives.

Focus on Private Sector-Led Growth:

With the state gradually retreating from non-strategic sectors, the private sector is expected to become the primary engine of growth. Investors should prioritize industries that complement this transition, such as export-oriented manufacturing, technology, and logistics.

Support Economic Diversification:

The government aims to reduce reliance on traditional sectors like energy and tourism by promoting growth in sectors such as renewable energy, industrial manufacturing, and agriculture technology. Initiatives like the Ras El-Hekma development project highlight opportunities in infrastructure and urban development.

Egypt's ambition to increase renewable energy's share to 42% of electricity generation by 2035 makes it an attractive destination for green investments.

Contribute to Sustainable Development:

Projects that emphasize environmental sustainability, social inclusion, and governance improvements can deliver both financial returns and long-term societal benefits. For example, investing in water management solutions, affordable housing, and education aligns with Egypt's sustainable development goals and offers avenues for impact-driven capital.

Navigate the Complex Regulatory Landscape

The regulatory environment in Egypt is evolving as part of its reform agenda. Understanding and adapting to these changes is critical for investors.

Understand the Evolving Regulatory Framework:

- Reforms such as the amended VAT law, expected by November 2024, aim to simplify tax compliance and reduce exemptions. While these reforms improve fiscal sustainability, they may also introduce transitional complexities for businesses.
- Investors should stay informed about labor laws, licensing requirements, and sector-specific regulations, especially in emerging industries like technology and renewable energy.

Partner with Local Expertise:

Navigating Egypt's regulatory and operational environment can be challenging for foreign investors. Collaborating with reputable local partners who possess strong expertise in compliance, legal frameworks, and market dynamics can mitigate risks and improve operational efficiency.

Engage with the Reform Agenda

Proactive engagement with Egypt's reform agenda can create synergies between public policy goals and private investment opportunities.

Advocate for Continued Reform Progress:

Investors should work with policymakers, industry associations, and other stakeholders to advocate for continued structural reforms that enhance the business environment. Areas like SOE transparency, competition policy, and trade facilitation are critical for leveling the playing field.

Active participation in policy dialogues can position investors as trusted stakeholders and align their ventures with national development priorities.

Support Initiatives that Promote Good Governance:

By adhering to high ethical standards and promoting **anti-corruption measures**, investors can contribute to improving governance practices. Supporting transparency initiatives, such as the **publication of aggregate SOE financial reports**, can help build trust and enhance market competitiveness.

Monitor Macroeconomic Developments

Given Egypt's dynamic economic environment, investors must remain agile and informed to navigate risks and seize emerging opportunities.

Stay Informed about Policy Changes:

Monitoring developments in inflation, exchange rate policy, and fiscal consolidation is essential. For example, Egypt's ongoing efforts to unify the exchange rate and phase out fuel subsidies by December 2025 will have significant implications for sectors reliant on imported goods or energy.

Develop Contingency Plans:

Investors should prepare for potential disruptions arising from global and regional uncertainties. Strategies might include hedging against currency risks, diversifying funding sources, or adjusting business models to account for potential fiscal tightening or rising borrowing costs.

Egypt's evolving economic landscape offers a mix of opportunities and challenges for investors. The government's ambitious reform agenda, including the divestment of SOEs, improvements to the regulatory environment, and fiscal consolidation, lays the foundation for long-term growth. However, risks such as geopolitical instability, inflation, and fiscal vulnerabilities necessitate a cautious and informed approach.

By conducting thorough risk assessments, prioritizing investments aligned with sustainable growth, navigating the regulatory landscape effectively, and engaging with the reform agenda, investors can position themselves for success in Egypt's dynamic market. A strategic, engaged, and flexible investment approach will be essential to unlocking the potential of this transforming economy.

Chapter Conclusion: Charting a Course Through Turbulent Waters: A Path to Sustainable Growth?

Egypt's economic journey is undoubtedly fraught with challenges. The confluence of global headwinds, regional instability, and domestic pressures has created a complex and uncertain landscape. High inflation, a substantial debt burden, and the lingering effects of external shocks continue to weigh on the economy.

Yet, amidst these challenges, a glimmer of hope emerges. The Egyptian government's commitment to its IMF-backed reform program, as evidenced by the recent exchange rate unification and decisive monetary policy tightening, is starting to yield positive results. Investor confidence is gradually returning, financing conditions are improving, and inflation is showing signs of abating.

The road ahead remains long and arduous. Fiscal consolidation requires a delicate balancing act between debt reduction and maintaining essential social spending. Structural reforms, while crucial for unlocking Egypt's long-term growth potential, face significant implementation challenges. The success of mega-projects like Ras El-Hekma hinges on careful planning and risk management.

For investors, Egypt presents a mixed bag of opportunities and risks. Thorough risk assessment, a focus on sustainable investments aligned with the country's development goals, and a deep understanding of the evolving regulatory landscape are paramount. Active engagement with the reform agenda and close monitoring of macroeconomic developments are essential for navigating this dynamic market.

Ultimately, Egypt's economic future hinges on the government's ability to maintain its commitment to reforms, effectively manage risks, and create a more conducive environment for private sector-led growth. The IMF report provides a valuable roadmap, but the journey requires sustained effort, resilience, and a clear vision for a more prosperous and inclusive Egypt.

Chapter (9)

Ethiopia: Balancing Economic Reforms with Growth Opportunities

"Its membership recognizes the rich multilateral contribution of Ethiopia to promote international peace, security and prosperity; and the continued commitment and leadership of Ethiopia to South-South cooperation"

Ethiopian Foreign Ministry

Ethiopia, a nation at the heart of the Horn of Africa, stands as a beacon of resilience and reform amidst significant economic challenges. With an expansive land area of 1,104,300 square kilometers, Ethiopia is the 27th largest country in the world, encompassing diverse landscapes ranging from the Ethiopian Highlands, Rift Valley, and Lake Tana (the source of the Blue Nile), to arid lowlands and fertile plains. These geographical features make Ethiopia not only a regional agricultural powerhouse but also a nation with vast hydropower potential, exemplified by the ambitious Grand Ethiopian Renaissance Dam (GERD), which aims to become Africa's largest hydroelectric facility.

Geography and Boundaries

Ethiopia is landlocked, bordered by six countries: Eritrea to the north, Djibouti and Somalia to the east, Kenya to the south, South Sudan to the west, and Sudan to the northwest. Its strategic location places it at the crossroads of the Middle East and East Africa, providing vital economic and geopolitical significance. Access to international trade routes is facilitated primarily through Djibouti's ports, underscoring Ethiopia's dependence on regional cooperation and infrastructure development.

Climate and Natural Resources

The country's tropical monsoon climate varies widely due to its topography, influencing its agricultural potential and economic activities. High-altitude regions, such as the Ethiopian Highlands, benefit from cooler temperatures and fertile soils ideal for crops like coffee, a leading export commodity. Lowland areas, characterized by arid conditions, present opportunities for livestock rearing and mineral exploration. Ethiopia's natural resources include small reserves of gold, platinum, copper, potash, and natural gas, as well as vast hydropower potential from its river systems.

Population and Regional Diversity

With a population exceeding 118 million and a growth rate of 2.37% (2024 estimate), Ethiopia is Africa's second-most populous country. The population is a mosaic of over 80 ethnic groups, the largest being Oromo (35.8%) and Amhara (24.1%), with other significant groups including Somali (7.2%), Tigray (5.7%), and Sidama (4.1%). This diversity extends to language and religion, with Amharic serving as the official national language and Oromo, Somali, and Tigrinya designated as regional working languages. Religious affiliations are similarly diverse, with Ethiopian Orthodox Christianity (43.8%) and Islam (31.3%) being the dominant faiths.

Key Differentiations and Strategic Importance

Ethiopia's historical legacy sets it apart from other African nations. As one of the only countries in Africa to resist full colonization (except for a brief Italian occupation from 1936–41), Ethiopia maintains a distinct identity rooted in its ancient monarchy and cultural heritage. Addis Ababa, the capital city and headquarters of the African Union, underscores Ethiopia's central role in regional diplomacy and its influence on the continent's political and economic integration.

Economic Significance of Geography

The varied geography and significant labor force provide opportunities and challenges. While fertile highlands support agriculture, arid regions are vulnerable to climate change, affecting food security and economic stability. Ethiopia's location near the Red Sea and Gulf of Aden enhances its potential as a regional trade hub, but the lack of direct access to ports necessitates heavy reliance on Djibouti for maritime trade.

This geographical and demographic richness, combined with Ethiopia's reform momentum, positions it as a key player in Africa's future, despite challenges such as poverty, resource scarcity, and systemic economic imbalances. These attributes underpin the nation's potential for sustained growth and development, particularly through targeted investment in infrastructure, agriculture, and energy sectors.

Economic Overview

GDP and Economic Reforms

Ethiopia's economy has been undergoing a transformative phase, supported by its Homegrown Economic Reform Agenda (HGER). Real GDP (Purchasing Power Parity): 2023: $354.604 billion, 2022: $332.968 billion and 2021: $316.145 billion while real GDP per capita (Purchasing Power Parity): 2023: $2,800 billion, 2022: $2,700 billion and 2021: $2,600 billion.

Real GDP growth, projected at 6.1% for 2023/24, highlights resilience despite global and local challenges such as inflation and foreign exchange constraints. The transition to a market-determined exchange rate regime in 2024 has marked a turning point, addressing longstanding external imbalances and facilitating currency stability. Although inflation remains high at 26.6% in 2023/24, the IMF projects moderation to single digits by 2028, driven by tight monetary policy and fiscal reforms.

Structural Contributions

Agriculture: Contributing over 30% to GDP, agriculture remains vital. Ethiopia exports coffee, gold, and cut flowers, with coffee alone accounting for a significant share of export revenue. Despite its importance, challenges such as water scarcity and reliance on traditional farming methods hinder potential.

Industry and Construction: Ethiopia's burgeoning construction sector, driven by public infrastructure projects, complements its industrial expansion. Notable projects include hydropower initiatives leveraging the nation's vast water resources.

Services: A growing sector, driven by finance, telecommunications, and logistics, supported by Ethiopia's regional importance as a trade hub accessing the Red Sea ports through Djibouti and Eritrea.

Trade and Investment

Export Profile

Ethiopia's exports reached **$10.865 billion in 2023**, reflecting a steady recovery from the disruptions caused by the COVID-19 pandemic, locust invasions, and internal conflicts. Coffee remains Ethiopia's leading export, accounting for a significant portion of foreign exchange earnings, followed by gold, garments, and cut flowers. These sectors not only underpin Ethiopia's trade portfolio but also provide critical employment opportunities in rural and urban areas.

The **United Arab Emirates (UAE)** is Ethiopia's largest export partner, accounting for **17% of exports**, driven primarily by the trade of gold and other precious metals. The **United States (13%)** and **Germany (6%)** follow as major destinations for Ethiopia's coffee, textiles, and cut flowers. Other key partners include **Saudi Arabia** and **Somalia**, reflecting Ethiopia's efforts to deepen ties with both regional and global markets.

Ethiopia has emphasized diversification of its export base to enhance economic resilience against external shocks. Recent policy reforms, such as currency liberalization and improved market access, aim to attract foreign investment into emerging sectors like manufacturing, renewable energy, and high-value agricultural exports. Additionally, the government is exploring opportunities to expand its share in global markets for processed goods, leveraging its large and low-cost labor force.

Import Reliance

Ethiopia's **imports totaled $22.951 billion in 2023**, highlighting a persistent trade deficit that underscores the country's dependence on external goods and capital inputs. Key imports include refined petroleum, essential for transportation and energy production, fertilizers, critical for agricultural productivity, and wheat, which supports food security amidst recurring droughts. Other significant imports include vaccines and palm oil, essential for healthcare and food processing.

China dominates Ethiopia's import landscape, supplying 24% of total imports, driven by the export of industrial machinery, electronics, and refined petroleum. The United States (9%) and India (8%) also play crucial roles, particularly in providing pharmaceuticals and agricultural inputs. Other notable partners include the UAE (6%) and the UK (4%), further reflecting Ethiopia's integration into diverse global supply chains.

Trade Challenges and Opportunities

Ethiopia's trade imbalance stems from a combination of factors, including limited export diversification, low value addition in key sectors, and reliance on imports for essential goods. However, ongoing economic reforms aim to address these challenges:

Export Diversification: Ethiopia's efforts to develop manufacturing industries, such as textiles and leather, are geared toward reducing over-reliance on primary commodities.

Infrastructure Investment: Improved transport and logistics infrastructure, including enhanced access to Djibouti's ports, are pivotal to facilitating trade and reducing costs.

Policy Reforms: The government's shift to a market-determined exchange rate and fiscal reforms are designed to enhance competitiveness and attract foreign direct investment (FDI).

While the trade deficit remains a pressing issue, Ethiopia's strategic location, growing labor force, and reform-oriented policies position it as a regional trade hub with significant potential for long-term economic growth and integration into global markets.

Investment Opportunities in Variety of sectors

Renewable Energy

Ethiopia boasts vast renewable energy potential, primarily driven by its abundant hydropower resources. The country is home to the Grand Ethiopian Renaissance Dam (GERD), expected to generate up to 6,450 MW upon completion, making it Africa's largest hydroelectric project. The government has also prioritized the development of solar and wind energy projects, leveraging its diverse climatic zones and open landscapes to diversify its energy mix.

Efforts to modernize Ethiopia's energy infrastructure include fostering public-private partnerships (PPPs). These partnerships aim to attract foreign investment and expertise to expand generation capacity, modernize transmission systems, and enhance rural electrification. Despite heavy reliance on hydropower, which accounts for over 90% of electricity production, the government targets a broader energy transition by increasing solar and wind contributions to meet growing domestic and regional energy demands.

Agriculture and Agribusiness

Agriculture remains the backbone of Ethiopia's economy, contributing 30% of GDP and employing a large portion of its labor force. However, challenges such as water scarcity, traditional farming practices, and climate vulnerability hinder productivity. Investments in irrigation systems, advanced farming technologies, and climate-resilient crops can unlock the sector's potential.

The government has prioritized high-value agricultural exports such as coffee, cut flowers, and vegetables. With coffee alone contributing a significant share of Ethiopia's $10.865 billion in exports (2023), there is ample room for investors to expand into value-added processing industries that enhance export competitiveness. Moreover, efforts to develop supply chain infrastructure and cold storage facilities for perishables present additional opportunities.

Infrastructure Development

Ethiopia's commitment to **infrastructure modernization** is evident in its ambitious public investment programs targeting railways, roads, and urban planning. Projects like the **Addis Ababa-Djibouti railway**, which facilitates trade with

Ethiopia's primary port, highlight the critical role of transportation in economic integration.

Urbanization, with 2.37% annual population growth, further necessitates infrastructure investments, including affordable housing, public transportation systems, and smart city technologies. These initiatives align with Ethiopia's vision of improving connectivity and supporting regional trade. The government's openness to PPP models ensures robust investment security, making this sector a focal point for domestic and international investors.

Digital Economy

Ethiopia's telecommunications sector is undergoing significant transformation, presenting a burgeoning opportunity for investors. The recent liberalization of the mobile market, marked by the entry of international operators like Safaricom, has energized the industry. With over 118 million people and a growing appetite for digital services, Ethiopia offers untapped potential in areas such as mobile broadband expansion, e-commerce platforms, and digital payment systems.

The government's focus on expanding fiber-optic networks and improving internet penetration complements its broader digital economy strategy. With just 1.31 million fixed broadband subscriptions in 2022, Ethiopia is ripe for investments in digital infrastructure and data center development to support growing demands for cloud computing and online services.

Trajectory and Vision for Investors

Ethiopia's trajectory reflects a balance between addressing systemic challenges and leveraging opportunities in its renewable energy, agriculture, infrastructure, and digital sectors. The government's reform agenda, coupled with growing regional integration and increasing foreign direct investment, positions Ethiopia as an attractive destination for long-term investment. By targeting strategic sectors and aligning with national priorities, investors can play a transformative role in the country's economic future

Economic Challenges and Policy Reforms

Inflation Control

Ethiopia's inflation, which averaged 26.6% in 2023/24, has been a significant challenge, impacting household purchasing power and macroeconomic stability. The National Bank of Ethiopia (NBE) has implemented a series of tight monetary policies to address inflationary pressures. These measures include raising interest rates, conducting regular open market operations (OMOs), and capping commercial bank lending growth to control liquidity.

From July to September 2024, the NBE conducted six liquidity-absorbing OMOs, withdrawing 135 billion birr (0.9% of GDP) from the market. This approach not only reduced excess liquidity but also signaled the central bank's commitment to maintaining price stability. Moreover, the government's decision to phase out monetary financing of fiscal deficits, a longstanding driver of inflation, has been critical in anchoring expectations.

The authorities plan to transition fully to an interest rate-based monetary policy framework by early 2025, ensuring positive real interest rates to further combat inflation. This reform is supported by clear communication strategies from the NBE to manage public expectations effectively.

Debt Sustainability

Ethiopia's public debt stood at **43.6% of GDP in 2024/25**, with external debt projected at **28.9% of GDP**. While these figures indicate a manageable trajectory compared to previous years, Ethiopia remains in external debt distress. To address this, the government has pursued a comprehensive **debt restructuring strategy** under the Common Framework, with active engagement from official creditors, including the Paris Club.

Efforts to restore debt sustainability focus on negotiating favorable terms with bilateral and commercial creditors. Key elements of this strategy include:

Reducing reliance on non-concessional borrowing: Apart from specific strategic projects like the Koysha Dam, Ethiopia has curtailed non-concessional external borrowing.

Strengthening debt management capacity: This includes improving transparency and implementing a robust debt management framework.

Restructuring external debt while maintaining fiscal discipline is critical to creating fiscal space for developmental priorities, such as infrastructure and social spending.

Foreign Exchange Reform

Ethiopia has made significant progress in addressing foreign exchange (FX) market distortions by transitioning to a floating exchange rate in July 2024. The reform eliminated the overvalued official exchange rate, narrowing the parallel market premium from 96% to around 5% within weeks.

Key measures implemented under the reform include:

- Abolishing restrictive current account controls.
- Allowing commercial banks to set FX rates within market-determined parameters.
- Enabling exporters to retain a portion of their FX earnings for longer durations, enhancing liquidity.

The new regime has improved transparency, reduced distortions, and bolstered investor confidence. As of late 2024, FX reserves had increased significantly, reaching $3.6 billion, up from $1.4 billion in June, due to higher gold export proceeds and international financial assistance.

However, challenges remain. Seasonal lows in export flows and unmet FX demand continue to pressure the market. To address these issues, the NBE has launched initiatives such as raising awareness among diaspora communities to boost remittances and ensuring efficient enforcement of FX market regulations.

Economic challenges and the HGER

Ethiopia's ability to tackle these economic challenges hinges on the sustained implementation of its Homegrown Economic Reform Agenda (HGER). Ethiopia's HGER, launched in

2019, is a comprehensive framework aimed at addressing the nation's macroeconomic vulnerabilities, promoting inclusive growth, and creating a competitive, private-sector-driven economy. This ambitious initiative seeks to rectify long-standing structural challenges while positioning Ethiopia as a regional economic hub. The HGER is built around three core pillars:

Macroeconomic Stability

The reform agenda prioritizes restoring fiscal and monetary balance to ensure economic resilience and stability. Key actions under this pillar include:

Fiscal Consolidation: Improving public financial management by enhancing revenue collection, curbing inefficient public spending, and reducing reliance on non-concessional external borrowing.

Monetary Policy Reforms: Shifting to an interest rate-based framework to control inflation and transitioning to a market-determined exchange rate to address foreign exchange imbalances.

Debt Management: Engaging in debt restructuring under the G20 Common Framework and strengthening domestic debt management capacity to ensure long-term sustainability.

These measures have already begun to yield results, such as narrowing the parallel market premium after the transition to a floating exchange rate in 2024 and a reduction in inflationary pressures.

Structural and Sectoral Reforms

The HGER emphasizes transformative reforms across key economic sectors to enhance productivity and competitiveness. Major initiatives include:

Liberalizing Key Sectors: Opening up previously state-dominated sectors, such as telecommunications, energy, and logistics, to private and foreign investors. The entry of Safaricom into Ethiopia's mobile market exemplifies the success of these liberalization efforts.

Agricultural Modernization: Introducing advanced technologies, improving irrigation systems, and enhancing value-added agricultural processing to increase productivity and export potential.

Energy Expansion: Leveraging Ethiopia's hydropower potential, including the Grand Ethiopian Renaissance Dam (GERD), and fostering the growth of solar and wind energy projects to diversify the energy mix.

These reforms aim to boost job creation, enhance export competitiveness, and reduce the economy's over-reliance on agriculture.

Private Sector-Led Growth

A key feature of the HGER is the shift toward a **private-sector-driven economy**, with a focus on improving the investment climate and fostering entrepreneurship. Specific reforms include:

Privatization and PPPs: Selling stakes in state-owned enterprises, such as Ethiopian Airlines and Ethio Telecom, and encouraging public-private partnerships in infrastructure and energy projects.

Ease of Doing Business: Simplifying regulatory processes, such as business registration and land acquisition, to attract foreign direct investment (FDI) and encourage domestic entrepreneurship.

Financial Sector Reform: Allowing foreign banks to operate in Ethiopia for the first time, a move designed to modernize the financial system, increase access to credit, and promote financial inclusion.

Cross-Cutting Themes

The HGER also emphasizes:

Job Creation: Addressing Ethiopia's youth unemployment challenge through skills development and expanding labor-intensive industries like manufacturing and agribusiness.

Social Inclusion and Safety Nets: Strengthening programs to reduce poverty and ensure that vulnerable populations benefit from economic reforms.

Climate Resilience: Incorporating sustainable practices into economic planning to mitigate the impacts of climate change, particularly in agriculture and energy.

While the HGER has achieved significant milestones, including economic stabilization and the attraction of global investors, challenges persist. Inflation remains high, debt levels require careful management, and political uncertainties can impact investor confidence. However, the agenda's robust framework and ongoing international support, including IMF funding, highlight Ethiopia's determination to build a resilient and inclusive economy.

The HGER represents Ethiopia's bold vision for transformation, reflecting its commitment to sustainable development, equitable growth, and global competitiveness. Its successful implementation will be critical for ensuring Ethiopia's emergence as a leading economic force in Africa.

Chapter Conclusion: Vision for the Future

Ethiopia stands at a transformative juncture, leveraging its geographical, demographic, and economic strengths to navigate challenges and unlock its immense growth potential. As the second-most populous country in Africa, its diverse population and rich cultural heritage form a strong foundation for fostering economic resilience and regional influence. The country's vast natural resources, ranging from fertile lands and hydropower capacity to mineral deposits, underscore its ability to drive sustainable growth through strategic investments.

Despite persistent challenges such as inflation, trade deficits, and external debt distress, Ethiopia's **Homegrown Economic Reform Agenda (HGER)** has laid the groundwork for meaningful progress. Key reforms, including the transition to a floating exchange rate, inflation control measures, and efforts to ensure debt sustainability, demonstrate the government's commitment to macroeconomic stability and structural transformation.

Investment opportunities abound across Ethiopia's critical sectors, including renewable energy, agriculture, infrastructure, and the burgeoning digital economy. Projects like the **Grand Ethiopian Renaissance Dam (GERD)**, advancements in irrigation and agribusiness, and the liberalization of telecommunications reflect a dynamic economy poised for integration into regional and global markets.

However, realizing Ethiopia's full potential requires sustained policy implementation, enhanced regional cooperation, and targeted investment in infrastructure and human capital. By addressing structural vulnerabilities and fostering an inclusive growth model, Ethiopia can position itself as a leading economic force in Africa, offering a wealth of opportunities for investors and development partners.

Ethiopia's journey of reform and resilience underscores its capacity to balance ambitious economic initiatives with the pressing need for social and environmental sustainability, charting a promising trajectory for the nation's future.

Chapter (10)

The UAE's Financial System: A Rock of Stability in Uncertain Times

"The UAE has consistently championed the value of multilateralism in supporting peace, security, and development globally"

Sheikh Abdullah bin Zayed Al Nahyan, UAE Minister of Foreign Affairs

The United Arab Emirates (UAE), strategically located at the southeastern tip of the Arabian Peninsula, serves as a vital crossroads connecting Europe, Asia, and Africa. Bordering Saudi Arabia to the south and Oman to the east, the UAE boasts an extensive coastline along the Persian Gulf and a prominent position near the Strait of Hormuz—a critical chokepoint for global energy trade. Encompassing a diverse geography that includes vast deserts, rugged mountains, and a thriving coastal plain, the UAE's landscape mirrors its dynamic economic and cultural identity. With a population of approximately **10 million**, largely concentrated in urban hubs like Dubai and Abu Dhabi, the UAE is a vibrant blend of Emirati traditions and a multinational workforce, fostering a unique environment for innovation, trade, and global connectivity. This strategic location and demographic diversity have established the UAE as a pivotal player in regional and international economic landscapes.

Beyond Oil: A Diversification Success Story

While hydrocarbons remain pivotal to the UAE's economy, its commitment to diversification has redefined its economic trajectory. UAE is a nation leveraging its resources, geographic advantages, and reform strategies to ensure sustainable and inclusive growth.

Non-Hydrocarbon Growth Achievements

Non-hydrocarbon GDP grew by **6.2% in 2023** and is projected to continue at **4.9% in 2024**, underscoring the UAE's economic transformation. This trajectory is bolstered by:

Robust Domestic Activity: Sectors like construction, financial services, and retail benefit from increased investments and consumer confidence. Business-friendly reforms further enhance activity.

Tourism Rebound: Dubai's recovery in luxury and mid-tier tourism reflects the UAE's strategic branding as a premier destination. Events like **COP28 in Dubai** have showcased the UAE's role in global climate action, boosting both regional and international tourism flows.

Capital Expenditure: Major infrastructure projects, including expansions in **renewable energy** and **transportation**, highlight the UAE's goal of becoming a global logistics and business hub.

Economic Diversification Drivers

The UAE's success in diversifying its economic portfolio stems from visionary policies:

Strategic Trade Agreements: The UAE has capitalized on Comprehensive Economic Partnership Agreements (CEPAs), enhancing trade ties with emerging economies while joining initiatives like the **India-Middle East-Europe Economic Corridor**, increasing global trade integration.

Advanced Manufacturing: Industries such as aerospace, renewable energy technologies, and petrochemicals have grown through targeted investments and innovation.

Sustainable Practices: Hosting global events like **COP28** has accelerated investments in solar energy and sustainable practices, complementing its ambitious **Net Zero by 2050** agenda.

Global Integration and Innovation

BRICS Membership: The UAE's accession to BRICS and deepening relationships with Asian economies strengthen its position in global value chains.

Tech Advancement: Government initiatives in AI and blockchain position the UAE as a leader in digital economies. Programs aimed at fostering **fintech ecosystems** attract international ventures and start-ups.

Unique Geographic and Social Advantages

The UAE's strategic location along the **Strait of Hormuz** is vital for global energy trade. With nearly **85% of its population concentrated in urban hubs like Dubai and Abu Dhabi**, the UAE maximizes efficiency in delivering infrastructure and services, ensuring rapid scalability for economic initiatives.

By seamlessly blending tradition with innovation, the UAE's diversification efforts not only reduce dependence on oil but also establish it as a leader in global economic, environmental, and technological landscapes.

Manufacturing: A Key Driver of Future Growth

Manufacturing continues to anchor the UAE's non-hydrocarbon economic strategy, driven by advancements in technology, diversification efforts, and global trade integration. Manufacturing has critical role in shaping the UAE's sustainable growth trajectory.

Downstream Hydrocarbon Industries

The UAE's hydrocarbon-related manufacturing, such as petrochemicals and refining, has seen substantial growth through investments in advanced processing technologies. These industries leverage the country's vast oil and gas reserves to create higher-value products for export markets, further enhancing fiscal revenues and global competitiveness. Emergence of non-hydrocarbon manufacturing

Non-hydrocarbon manufacturing is rapidly expanding, with **renewable energy technologies**, **aerospace**, and **electric vehicles (EVs)** leading the charge. The UAE has prioritized investments in **solar panel production facilities**, reflecting its commitment to renewable energy and climate goals.

High-tech manufacturing, including **3D printing** and **smart industrial solutions**, is gaining traction, fueled by government incentives and innovation hubs like Abu Dhabi's **Khalifa Industrial Zone (KIZAD)** and Dubai's **Tech District**.

Key Initiatives Supporting Diversification

The UAE's diversification efforts are underpinned by strategic initiatives that enhance its economic resilience and global integration. This section sheds light on the multifaceted approaches driving the UAE's transformation into a diversified and sustainable economy.

Comprehensive Economic Partnership Agreements (CEPAs)

The UAE has solidified its position as a global trade hub through Comprehensive Economic Partnership Agreements (CEPAs) with key partners, including India, Israel, and Indonesia. These agreements reduce trade barriers, streamline logistics, and boost exports across sectors such as manufacturing, technology, and agriculture.

CEPAs enable the UAE to leverage its strategic location at the crossroads of major trade routes, enhancing its integration into global supply chains and expanding market access for local businesses.

The UAE's membership in BRICS further deepens its trade relations with emerging economies, complementing the objectives of CEPAs to diversify trading partners and reduce dependency on traditional markets.

Digitalization: Transforming the Economy

The UAE's heavy investments in cutting-edge digital technologies are reshaping its economy:

Artificial Intelligence (AI): The UAE is a global leader in AI, evidenced by initiatives like the National AI Strategy 2031, which integrates AI across industries such as healthcare, logistics, and energy.

Blockchain and Fintech: Dubai and Abu Dhabi have become fintech hubs, attracting global startups and fostering blockchain-based applications for banking, logistics, and government services.

Smart Cities: Initiatives such as Dubai Smart City and Abu Dhabi's Hub71 focus on integrating IoT (Internet of Things) technologies, enabling efficient urban planning and resource management.

Digital transformation efforts are supported by investments in robust infrastructure, including 5G networks and data centers, which provide a solid foundation for future technological advancements.

Green Initiatives: A Global Leader in Sustainability

The UAE's leadership in renewable energy and sustainable practices reflects its commitment to combating climate change while driving economic growth:

Renewable Energy Projects: The UAE hosts some of the world's largest renewable energy facilities, such as the Mohammed bin Rashid Al Maktoum Solar Park and plans to triple renewable energy capacity by 2030.

Green Hydrogen: Investments in green hydrogen production are positioning the UAE as a global hub for clean energy, catering to growing international demand.

Sustainability Finance: The UAE has developed a comprehensive green finance ecosystem, including the issuance of green bonds and sustainability-linked loans, to fund eco-friendly projects.

COP28 Leadership: As the host of COP28, the UAE has reinforced its role in advancing global climate action and mobilizing investments in clean energy.

Holistic Diversification Approach

- The UAE's "Operation 300bn" initiative aims to increase the contribution of the industrial sector to GDP, fostering innovation and reducing reliance on imports.
- Efforts to nurture talent through programs such as the UAE National Innovation Strategy and investments in research and development (R&D) ensure a skilled workforce aligned with future economic needs.

- The "Make it in the Emirates" campaign further emphasizes industrial self-reliance while attracting international investors to key manufacturing sectors.

By prioritizing trade, digitalization, and sustainability, the UAE has established itself as a model of diversification and innovation, creating an economic ecosystem resilient to global **challenges and attractive to investors worldwide.**

A Hub for Innovation and Investment

The UAE has solidified its position as a global destination for innovation and investment, attracting significant international interest through strategic initiatives and robust economic policies. The UAE's appeal stems from its business-friendly environment, advanced infrastructure, innovation leadership, and commitment to sustainability.

The UAE's regulatory reforms have been pivotal in enhancing its investment landscape:

Ease of Doing Business: Policies simplifying company registration, reducing bureaucratic barriers, and offering 100% foreign ownership in many sectors make the UAE highly attractive to investors.

Tax Incentives: The introduction of **corporate income tax at a competitive 9% rate** is complemented by the absence of personal income tax, reinforcing its appeal to businesses and individuals.

Economic Free Zones: Over **40 specialized free zones** provide tailored incentives, such as tax exemptions, streamlined customs, and sector-specific infrastructure, fostering industry growth in areas like technology, finance, and logistics.

Strategic Location and Infrastructure

Situated at the crossroads of Europe, Asia, and Africa, the UAE leverages its **geographical advantage** for global connectivity:

- **World-Class Ports and Airports:** The UAE is home to **Jebel Ali Port**, one of the largest and most efficient ports globally, and **Dubai International Airport**, a major hub for passenger and cargo traffic.
- **Global Trade Integration:** Strategic trade agreements like CEPAs and partnerships through organizations like **BRICS** enable businesses to access emerging and established markets with reduced tariffs and seamless logistics.
- **Future-Ready Infrastructure:** Investments in **hyperloop technology**, **autonomous vehicles**, and **smart logistics networks** highlight the UAE's commitment to staying at the forefront of global transportation innovations.

The UAE has positioned itself as a leader in fostering innovation:

Artificial Intelligence and R&D: The UAE's **National Artificial Intelligence Strategy 2031** focuses on integrating AI across key sectors like healthcare, logistics, and governance. Abu Dhabi's **Hub71** and Dubai's **Area 2071** serve as innovation hubs supporting tech start-ups.

Start-Up Support: Programs like Dubai Future Accelerators and Sharjah Research Technology and Innovation Park offer funding, mentorship, and infrastructure to foster entrepreneurial growth.

Global Collaboration: The UAE actively collaborates with international research institutions and private enterprises to drive innovation in emerging fields like quantum computing, space exploration, and biotechnology.

Investor Confidence

The IMF underscores the UAE's ability to attract safe-haven inflows and conduct successful Initial Public Offerings (IPOs), even amidst global economic volatility:

Safe-Haven Inflows: The UAE's stable political environment, well-regulated financial system, and currency peg to the US dollar provide a secure environment for investors.

IPO Success Stories: Recent IPOs in sectors like logistics, energy, and technology have drawn strong demand from institutional and retail investors globally, highlighting the UAE's economic vibrancy and growth prospects.

By integrating forward-looking policies, cutting-edge technologies, and sustainable practices, the UAE has established itself as a beacon for global innovation and investment. This proactive approach ensures that the nation remains resilient and attractive to businesses and investors in a rapidly changing global landscape.

Navigating the Fiscal Landscape

The UAE's fiscal landscape demonstrates a strong foundation, rooted in prudent management and forward-thinking policies. The UAE continues to showcase resilience in its fiscal policies while advancing structural reforms to ensure long-term sustainability.

Fiscal Sustainability

Stable Surpluses: The UAE's general government fiscal surpluses are projected to average **4.3% of GDP through the medium term**, reflecting a strong fiscal position bolstered by elevated oil prices and controlled spending.

Declining Deficits: the non-hydrocarbon primary deficit is projected to decline to **20.4% of non-hydrocarbon GDP** during the 2023–2027 period, reflecting the UAE's ongoing fiscal reforms and diversification efforts. This marks an improvement of approximately **2.2 percentage points** compared to earlier projections, largely due to:

- The introduction of **corporate income tax (CIT)** in 2023.
- Enhanced non-hydrocarbon revenue collection efforts.
- Efforts to rationalize spending and phase out subsidies.

The steady reduction in this deficit underscores the UAE's commitment to long-term fiscal sustainability and reduced reliance on hydrocarbon revenues, aligning with its diversification strategy and economic resilience goals.

Prudent Debt Management: With government debt declining to an estimated **31.3% of GDP in 2024**, the UAE demonstrates its ability to manage fiscal risks while maintaining ample fiscal buffers.

Broader Revenue Base

Corporate Income Tax: The UAE's introduction of a **corporate income tax in 2023** is a milestone in broadening its revenue base. At a globally competitive rate of 9%, this measure aligns with international tax standards while preserving the country's appeal as a business hub.

Potential Tax Expansions: The UAE is exploring additional non-hydrocarbon revenue sources, such as property and green taxes, to further diversify its fiscal streams in line with its **Net Zero by 2050** commitments.

Improved Tax Collection: Leveraging technology and streamlined processes, the UAE is enhancing tax compliance and reducing evasion, ensuring the efficient collection of fiscal revenues.

Enhanced Spending Efficiency

Subsidy Reform: The UAE has undertaken significant steps to reform its subsidy framework, particularly targeting subsidies in the **energy and water sectors**, which have historically accounted for a notable portion of government expenditures. According to the **IMF 2024 Article IV Report,** subsidies related to energy, water, and fuel were estimated at approximately **AED 15-20 billion ($4.1-$5.5 billion)** annually in recent years. These subsidies were provided to ensure affordability for households and businesses but have posed challenges to fiscal efficiency and sustainability.

In response, the UAE has initiated a **gradual phase-out of subsidies**:

- **Energy Subsidies:** Electricity and fuel prices have been partially deregulated, with fuel prices now adjusted monthly based on global market trends. This reform aligns energy costs more closely with actual market values, reducing fiscal burdens and promoting responsible energy consumption.
- **Water Subsidies:** Efforts are underway to align water tariffs with the true cost of production and supply, encouraging water conservation and sustainable usage, especially critical in the UAE's arid climate.
- **Environmental Objectives:** Phasing out subsidies also supports the UAE's **Net Zero 2050 Strategy**, incentivizing investments in renewable energy and energy-efficient technologies.

Targeted Social Safety Nets: Complementing subsidy reforms, the UAE is strengthening social safety nets, ensuring vulnerable populations are supported through expanded welfare programs and healthcare access.

Growth-Friendly Consolidation: Fiscal consolidation measures focus on balancing expenditure control with investment in growth-oriented sectors like infrastructure, digital transformation, and renewable energy.

Structural Reforms and Transparency

Transparency and Governance: The UAE is advancing fiscal transparency through enhanced reporting mechanisms and public financial management reforms.

Public Debt Markets: Successful issuance of **domestic and international bonds**, such as the $7 billion raised in international markets, reflects robust investor confidence in the UAE's fiscal strength.

By prioritizing sustainability, diversification, and efficiency, the UAE is navigating its fiscal landscape with confidence. These strategic measures not only enhance economic resilience but also reinforce the nation's position as a global leader in fiscal prudence and innovation.

A Secure and Stable Financial System

The UAE's financial system stands as a pillar of resilience, marked by robust regulatory frameworks, a sound banking sector, and proactive oversight. UAE is committed to ensuring financial stability amidst evolving global challenges.

Banking Sector Stability

Strong Metrics: The UAE's banking sector exhibits **strong financial metrics**, reflecting its resilience and adherence to regulatory standards set by the **Central Bank of the UAE (CBUAE)**. Key ratios include:

Capital Adequacy Ratios (CAR): The **CAR** for UAE banks consistently exceeds the **Basel III requirements** and the CBUAE's regulatory minimum of **13%**, including a 3% capital conservation buffer.

As of 2023, the average CAR for UAE banks stood at approximately **17%-18%**, highlighting strong capitalization and the ability to absorb financial shocks.

Liquidity Coverage Ratio (LCR): The **LCR** measures a bank's ability to meet short-term obligations using high-quality liquid assets. UAE banks maintain an LCR well above the CBUAE's minimum requirement of **100%**, averaging around **160%-180%** in recent years.

Net Stable Funding Ratio (NSFR): The **NSFR** ensures that banks maintain a stable funding profile over a one-year horizon. UAE banks consistently meet or exceed the Basel III requirement of **100%**, with many banks achieving an NSFR of approximately **110%-120%**.

These metrics underscore the soundness of the UAE banking system, which benefits from proactive regulatory oversight and prudent risk management practices. These strengths support confidence in the financial sector and its capacity to withstand economic or financial disruptions.

Improved Profitability: Higher interest rates and steady credit growth have bolstered bank profitability. The **IMF 2024 Article IV Report** highlights that higher interest rates and steady credit growth significantly boosted bank profitability in the UAE. Specifically, **net interest income contributed an estimated AED 17 billion ($4.6 billion)** in additional earnings to UAE banks' balance sheets in 2023, reflecting a substantial year-over-year increase. This improvement underscores the strong positive impact of rising interest margins on the financial sector's overall performance.

Digital Banking Evolution: The UAE continues to modernize its banking sector, integrating **fintech innovations** and enhancing customer access through digital platforms, further reinforcing the sector's competitiveness.

Real Estate Oversight

Critical Vulnerabilities: Real estate remains a significant area of exposure for UAE banks, with potential risks from price volatility and over-leverage in certain segments.

Regulatory Measures: The **Central Bank of the UAE (CBUAE)** has implemented several measures and requirements to strengthen prudential regulations and manage risks in the real estate sector. These include:

- **Loan-to-Value (LTV) Ratios:** The CBUAE has set maximum LTV limits for mortgages to prevent over-leveraging by borrowers and excessive exposure by banks. For example:
- **First-time homebuyers:** A cap of **80% LTV** for UAE nationals and **75% LTV** for expatriates.
- **Investment properties:** A stricter limit of **65%-70% LTV**, depending on the property type.

For properties priced above AED 5 million, LTV ratios are further reduced to encourage responsible borrowing.

Stress-Testing Requirements:

Banks are required to conduct **regular stress tests** to assess their ability to withstand shocks, such as significant declines in property prices or increases in interest rates.

These stress tests evaluate the impact on capital adequacy and liquidity under adverse scenarios, ensuring that banks maintain resilience during economic downturns.

Caps on Debt Service-to-Income (DSTI) Ratios:

To protect borrowers from overextending financially, the CBUAE mandates that monthly mortgage payments cannot exceed a certain percentage of the borrower's income, typically capped at **50%-60% of gross monthly income**.

Risk Weighting for Real Estate Loans:

The CBUAE requires banks to apply **higher risk weights** to real estate loans in their capital adequacy calculations. This ensures that banks allocate sufficient capital to cover potential losses from property sector exposures.

Increased Oversight of Valuations:

Banks must adhere to strict guidelines for **property valuations**, requiring independent appraisals to prevent inflated loan amounts based on overestimated property values.

Limits on Exposure to Real Estate:

The CBUAE has imposed caps on the total exposure banks can have to the real estate sector as a proportion of their loan portfolios. For instance, banks must ensure that their real estate lending does not disproportionately exceed their overall risk appetite.

By enforcing these measures, the CBUAE mitigates systemic risks and promotes stability in the financial sector, ensuring a balanced approach to growth in the real estate market.

Market Monitoring: Continued close monitoring of real estate dynamics is vital, particularly in high-growth emirates like Dubai and Abu Dhabi, to prevent systemic vulnerabilities.

AML/CFT Framework Progress

FATF "Grey List" Removal: In 2024, the UAE successfully exited the Financial Action Task Force (FATF) "grey list", demonstrating substantial progress in enhancing its Anti-Money Laundering and Combating the Financing of Terrorism (AML/CFT) framework.

Strengthened Oversight: The UAE has implemented stricter beneficial ownership regulations, enhanced transparency in corporate structures, and improved enforcement mechanisms against illicit financial activities.

International Cooperation: Increased collaboration with international organizations and financial intelligence units has further elevated the UAE's ability to combat financial crimes effectively.

Additional Measures Supporting Financial Stability

- **Macroprudential Oversight:** The CBUAE continues to enforce macroprudential measures, including regular stress tests and scenario analyses, to ensure financial system resilience under adverse economic conditions.
- **Addressing Nonperforming Loans (NPLs):** While NPL ratios have declined from pandemic peaks, it is vital to continue provisioning and proactive managing of legacy NPLs to safeguard banking sector health.
- **Digital and Fintech Regulation:** As the UAE embraces digital innovation, the CBUAE has developed robust frameworks for supervising **fintech activities**, ensuring a balance between fostering innovation and mitigating risks like data breaches and cyberattacks.

Global Financial Integration

Capital Markets Expansion: The UAE has significantly enhanced its capital markets, making them more attractive to international investors. A key driver of this expansion has been the success of Initial Public Offerings (IPOs), which have collectively raised billions of dollars in recent years. In 2023 alone, the UAE saw IPOs raise an estimated $8 billion, reflecting strong demand from both domestic and global institutional investors. Notable IPOs include Borouge, the petrochemicals giant, which raised $2 billion, and DEWA (Dubai Electricity and Water Authority), which brought in $6.1 billion—the largest public offering in the UAE's history.

In addition to equity markets, the UAE has developed a more liquid bond market, with substantial issuances of green bonds and conventional debt securities. These developments are supported by regulatory reforms aimed at increasing transparency and efficiency in the capital markets, such as enhancements in disclosure requirements and investor protections.

The expansion of the UAE's capital markets underscores the confidence international investors have in the country's economic stability and growth trajectory, positioning the UAE as a leading financial hub in the region.

Safe-Haven Appeal: Amid global economic volatility, the UAE remains a safe haven for investors, thanks to its currency peg to the US dollar, political stability, and well-regulated financial environment.

Sustainability in Finance

Green Finance Leadership: The UAE is developing its green finance capabilities, including the issuance of green and sustainability-linked bonds, to align financial markets with its environmental goals.

Climate Risk Assessments: The CBUAE has begun integrating climate-related financial risks into its supervisory frameworks, reflecting its commitment to sustainability in the financial sector.

By combining strong regulatory oversight, innovation in banking and fintech, and a commitment to combating financial crimes, the UAE's financial system remains robust and globally competitive. These efforts not only enhance financial stability but also reinforce the nation's reputation as a reliable and attractive destination for global capital.

Opportunities Amidst Transformation

The UAE's economic transformation presents a wealth of emerging opportunities for investors, underpinned by its forward-looking strategies and dynamic market landscape. The following highlights areas ripe for investment that align with the UAE's vision for sustainable, diversified growth.

Digitalization: A Growing Ecosystem

- **Smart Government Initiatives:** The UAE's Smart Dubai and Digital Abu Dhabi initiatives have created a seamless digital government infrastructure, streamlining services and enabling greater transparency, which fosters investor confidence.
- **Artificial Intelligence (AI):** The UAE's leadership in AI through its National AI Strategy 2031 has encouraged significant investments in industries such as healthcare, logistics, and autonomous systems.
- **E-Commerce Boom:** The growth of digital marketplaces and consumer adoption of online platforms are supported by cutting-edge logistics

networks and advanced payment systems, creating new opportunities for retail and tech-based solutions.

Green Energy Transition: A Leader in Clean Energy

- **Hydrogen Economy:** The UAE is positioning itself as a global hub for green hydrogen production, with projects like the Masdar Green Hydrogen Plant aimed at exporting clean energy to international markets.
- **Renewable Energy Expansion:** The UAE's solar power initiatives, including significant capacity additions at the **Mohammed bin Rashid Al Maktoum Solar Park**, aim to triple renewable energy output by 2030, providing opportunities for developers and investors in clean energy infrastructure.
- **Energy Efficiency Solutions:** Programs to retrofit buildings with energy-efficient technologies and establish **green cities** like Masdar City are opening avenues for green technology providers and sustainability-focused investments.

Trade and Tourism: Global Connectivity

- **Logistics Hub Development:** Investments in state-of-the-art ports like Jebel Ali and airport expansions are positioning the UAE as a major global logistics hub, creating opportunities in freight forwarding, warehousing, and supply chain optimization.
- **Tourism Diversification:** Beyond luxury offerings, the UAE is expanding into eco-tourism and cultural

tourism, with projects such as Al Ain's Heritage Revival Plan and wildlife conservation parks designed to attract environmentally conscious travelers.

- **Major Events:** The UAE's hosting of international events like COP28 has further elevated its profile as a destination for business and leisure, driving demand for related hospitality, travel, and event management services.

Advanced Manufacturing and Technology

Industrial Growth: The UAE's Operation 300bn aims to elevate manufacturing's contribution to GDP, targeting sectors such as advanced materials, aerospace, and precision engineering.

Tech Innovation: The integration of 3D printing, robotics, and IoT solutions in manufacturing processes enhances efficiency, creating opportunities for investors in industrial automation technologies.

Free Zones for Industry: Special economic zones like KIZAD and Dubai South offer tax incentives, world-class infrastructure, and export facilitation for manufacturing ventures.

Financial Services Evolution

Fintech Opportunities: With its growing reputation as a regional fintech hub, the UAE offers fertile ground for start-ups in mobile banking, blockchain, and insurtech. The introduction of **digital currency frameworks** by the Central Bank further enhances opportunities in this space.

Sustainability Finance: The UAE's issuance of **green bonds** and development of regulatory frameworks for sustainable investments provide significant opportunities for international financial institutions and private investors.

Healthcare and Biotechnology

Health Innovation: Investments in biotechnology, genomics, and telemedicine are growing, driven by government-backed R&D programs and initiatives such as Abu Dhabi's Biotech Hub.

Medical Tourism: The UAE is capitalizing on its world-class healthcare facilities and strategic location to attract patients from across the globe, creating opportunities for investors in specialized healthcare services and medical infrastructure.

By leveraging its strategic location, proactive policies, and commitment to innovation and sustainability, the UAE continues to present unparalleled opportunities for investors seeking to capitalize on its dynamic transformation. These initiatives align with the UAE's long-term vision, ensuring that investments contribute to a resilient and sustainable future.

Key Takeaways for Investors

The UAE's evolving economic landscape offers substantial opportunities for investors, but a nuanced and informed approach is essential to navigate its dynamic environment effectively. Key considerations for investors are outlined below:

Strategic Partnerships

Localized Expertise: Partnering with local stakeholders, including government entities, Emirati businesses, and free zone authorities, ensures a deeper understanding of regulatory requirements and market dynamics.

Cultural Alignment: Building strong relationships based on cultural awareness and trust is critical for successful collaborations, particularly in sectors such as tourism, real estate, and advanced manufacturing.

Public-Private Collaboration: Government-backed programs, such as the **Make it in the Emirates initiative**, encourage private sector participation in strategic sectors like green energy and high-tech manufacturing.

Alignment with the UAE's 2050 Strategies

Green Energy Transition: Investments aligned with the UAE's **Net Zero 2050 Strategy**, such as renewable energy infrastructure and green finance initiatives, are likely to receive robust government support.

Digital Transformation: Projects that integrate advanced technologies like **AI, blockchain, and IoT** in priority sectors, such as healthcare and logistics, resonate with the UAE's broader innovation agenda.

Sectoral Growth: Key industries identified in the **Operation 300bn strategy**, the "**Operation 300bn**" initiative is a comprehensive industrial strategy launched by the UAE government to bolster the country's industrial sector and diversify its economy. The initiative is named after its ambitious goal of increasing the industrial sector's contribution to GDP to AED 300 billion (approximately $82 billion) by 2031, up from AED 133 billion ($36 billion) in 2021. Key objectives are:

Economic Diversification: Reduce reliance on oil revenues by fostering growth in non-hydrocarbon sectors, particularly manufacturing and advanced industries.

Promoting Industrial Growth: Develop high-value industries such as aerospace, pharmaceuticals, clean energy technologies, and advanced manufacturing.

Encourage local production and reduce dependency on imports for essential goods and services.

Creating Job Opportunities: Build a knowledge-based economy by generating skilled jobs, with a focus on STEM (science, technology, engineering, and mathematics) fields.

Support for SMEs and Innovation: Empower **small and medium-sized enterprises (SMEs)** by providing financial, technical, and regulatory support.

Foster innovation and investment in **research and development (R&D)** to position the UAE as a global industrial and technological leader.

Sustainability Goals: Align industrial growth with environmental objectives, promoting **green technologies** and

energy-efficient practices in line with the UAE's **Net Zero 2050 Strategy**.

The initiative is spearheaded by the **Ministry of Industry and Advanced Technology (MoIAT)** and supported by incentives like:

- Access to **special economic zones**.
- Subsidized financing through programs like the Emirates Development Bank (EDB).
- Regulatory reforms to attract foreign and local investments.

Risk Assessment and Mitigation

Global Economic Volatility: The UAE's openness to global trade and investment makes it susceptible to external shocks. Investors should assess how potential downturns in global growth or financial markets may impact their operations.

Energy Transition Risks: While the UAE is a leader in renewable energy, the global shift away from hydrocarbons poses risks to certain traditional industries. Diversifying portfolios into emerging sectors can offset these challenges.

Regulatory Adaptation: As the UAE continues to modernize its fiscal and regulatory systems, including tax reforms, investors should remain agile and adapt to evolving frameworks to maintain compliance and competitiveness.

Leveraging Free Zones and Infrastructure

Special Economic Zones: Free zones like **Jebel Ali Free Zone (JAFZA)** and **Khalifa Industrial Zone Abu Dhabi (KIZAD)** offer targeted incentives such as zero taxation, world-class infrastructure, and streamlined customs processes, providing a strong base for regional and global operations.

Global Connectivity: The UAE's superior logistics network, supported by **state-of-the-art ports and airports**, ensures efficient supply chain management and market access, which are critical for export-driven industries.

Talent and Innovation Focus

Access to Skilled Workforce: The UAE's investments in education, research hubs, and partnerships with global universities have cultivated a skilled, multinational talent pool, especially in high-growth sectors like technology and finance.

Innovation Hubs: Government initiatives such as **Hub71 in Abu Dhabi** and **Dubai Internet City** provide an ecosystem for start-ups and tech companies to thrive, backed by funding, mentorship, and infrastructure support.

Strategic Diversification Across Markets

Broader Revenue Streams: The UAE's diversification into non-hydrocarbon sectors, including tourism, financial services, and digital economies, offers resilient growth opportunities that are less dependent on oil market fluctuations.

Regional Integration: As part of **BRICS** and through Comprehensive Economic Partnership Agreements (CEPAs), the UAE facilitates access to emerging markets, expanding opportunities for international trade and investment.

By leveraging strategic partnerships, aligning with the UAE's forward-looking policies, and proactively managing risks, investors can capitalize on the UAE's robust economic transformation. The nation's unique blend of global connectivity, innovative ecosystems, and government-backed initiatives provides a fertile ground for sustainable and profitable investments.

Chapter Conclusion: A Vision of Stability and Opportunity

The UAE's financial system and broader economic landscape exemplify resilience, strategic foresight, and innovation in navigating a complex global environment. The UAE's ability to sustain stability while embracing transformative growth across diverse sectors is vital.

The UAE's diversification beyond hydrocarbons reflects a deliberate strategy to future-proof its economy. By prioritizing non-hydrocarbon growth through robust domestic activity, tourism recovery, and capital expenditure in infrastructure and renewable energy, the nation has redefined its economic trajectory. Initiatives like the **Operation 300bn** industrial strategy, **Comprehensive Economic Partnership Agreements (CEPAs)**, and advanced manufacturing advancements emphasize its role as a global trade and innovation hub.

The UAE's fiscal prudence remains a cornerstone of its stability. The introduction of a corporate income tax, subsidy reforms, and enhanced spending efficiency signal a commitment to financial sustainability while supporting growth-friendly investments. The country's ability to maintain substantial fiscal surpluses and reduce its reliance on hydrocarbon revenues reflects its forward-thinking governance.

Its financial system continues to attract international confidence, supported by a robust regulatory framework, well-capitalized banks, and advancements in fintech and digital banking. The removal of the UAE from the **FATF grey list** underscores its progress in combating financial crimes, further solidifying its reputation as a secure and transparent financial hub.

For investors, the UAE offers unparalleled opportunities in digital transformation, green energy, advanced manufacturing, and global trade. Its strategic location, state-of-the-art infrastructure, and innovation-driven economy provide a strong foundation for sustainable growth. Moreover, initiatives like **Hub71** and **Dubai Future Accelerators** demonstrate the UAE's commitment to fostering a dynamic ecosystem for entrepreneurs and global corporations alike.

As the UAE aligns with its **Net Zero 2050 Strategy**, it not only sets a benchmark for sustainable development but also positions itself as a global leader in renewable energy and green finance. The hosting of **COP28** and investments in green hydrogen and solar energy highlight its proactive stance on climate action, further bolstering its global standing.

In conclusion, the UAE's financial system and economic strategy serve as a beacon of stability and opportunity in uncertain times. Its ability to blend fiscal prudence with ambitious growth initiatives provides a compelling narrative for investors and stakeholders. By continuing to leverage its geographic, economic, and technological strengths, the UAE is poised to maintain its trajectory as a global powerhouse, creating value for its people and the international community.

Chapter (11)

Indonesia Economic Outlook: Growth, Debt, and the Road to High-Income Status

"A strategic way to increase collaboration and partnership with other developing nations"

Indonesia's Foreign Minister

Indonesia, the largest economy in Southeast Asia, has been navigating a complex set of global challenges and domestic reforms. As the country aims to transition to a high-income status by 2045, it faces a delicate balancing act between pursuing growth and maintaining fiscal and financial stability. This chapter highlights Indonesia's robust economic performance, resilience against external shocks, and the pivotal role of structural reforms in shaping the future.

Spanning across an archipelago of 13,466 islands, Indonesia occupies a strategic location between the Indian and Pacific Oceans, serving as a vital maritime hub for global trade. With a total land area of 1.9 million square kilometers and a coastline stretching 54,716 km, the country is the world's largest island nation. Its unique topography includes vast coastal lowlands and interior mountain ranges, with Puncak Jaya standing as the highest peak at 4,884 meters. Indonesia is also home to the largest number of active volcanoes globally, forming part of the Pacific "Ring of Fire," which makes it prone to seismic activity, including earthquakes and tsunamis.

Indonesia's tropical climate, rich biodiversity, and extensive natural resources—including petroleum, natural gas, tin, nickel, bauxite, copper, coal, gold, and timber—offer significant economic opportunities but also pose sustainability challenges. The country is a global leader in nickel production, a critical component in battery manufacturing, making it an essential player in the energy transition.

With a population of approximately 281 million in 2024, Indonesia ranks as the fourth most populous nation globally and the world's largest Muslim-majority country. The demographic composition is diverse, comprising over 300 ethnic groups, with Javanese being the dominant ethnicity (40.1%). The majority of the population is concentrated on the island of Java, making it one of the most densely populated regions in the world. The urbanization rate is increasing, with 58.6% of the population residing in cities.

GDP Growth: Resilient but Constrained by External Headwinds

Indonesia's economy continues to demonstrate robust resilience despite an increasingly challenging global landscape. In 2023, real GDP growth reached 5.0%, a slight moderation from the 5.3% recorded in 2022, reflecting the economy's ability to sustain momentum amid external pressures. Growth is projected to remain steady at 5.0% in 2024 before inching up to 5.1% in 2025, driven primarily by strong domestic demand. The nominal GDP figures for recent years based on IMF data are:

- 2022: IDR 19,588 trillion (~USD 1.29 trillion)
- 2023: IDR 20,892 trillion (~USD 1.37 trillion)
- 2024 (Projected): IDR 22,555 trillion (~USD 1.47 trillion)
- 2025 (Projected): IDR 24,367 trillion (~USD 1.58 trillion)
- 2026 (Projected): IDR 26,274 trillion (~USD 1.70 trillion)
- 2027 (Projected): IDR 28,313 trillion (~USD 1.83 trillion)

Private consumption, a key pillar of economic activity, is expected to expand by 4.9% in 2024 and 5.1% in 2025, supported by rising incomes, a growing middle class, and stable inflation. Government consumption, which rebounded in 2023, is also expected to contribute positively, particularly through public infrastructure projects. Meanwhile, gross fixed capital formation—an indicator of investment—will grow by an estimated 4.4% in 2024 and accelerate to 5.0% in 2025, reflecting investor confidence and ongoing economic reforms.

However, Indonesia's external sector presents notable risks. While the country remains a major exporter of commodities such as coal, palm oil, and base metals, declining global demand and falling commodity prices have softened export growth. In 2022, net exports made a significant contribution of 0.8 percentage points to GDP growth, but this support is expected to diminish over the medium term. The slowing of Indonesia's key trading partners—especially China, the United States, and major European economies—has weighed on external demand. Additionally, the global financial environment, characterized by elevated interest rates in advanced economies, has led to capital flow volatility, affecting Indonesia's exchange rate stability and external financing conditions.

These factors have led to a shift in Indonesia's external balance. The current account, which posted a modest surplus of 1.0% of GDP in 2022, swung into a small deficit of 0.1% in 2023 and is projected to widen further to -0.9% of GDP in 2024. This deterioration is largely attributed to weaker export earnings, as well as the gradual recovery of imports, which are expected to rise in tandem with domestic demand. Nonetheless, foreign direct investment (FDI) inflows have remained stable, helping to support Indonesia's balance of payments and foreign exchange reserves.

Despite these external constraints, Indonesia's overall growth outlook remains optimistic. Domestic economic activity continues to be resilient, bolstered by rising consumer confidence, increased infrastructure spending, and ongoing structural reforms aimed at enhancing the investment climate. The output gap, which was estimated at -0.3% of GDP in 2023, is expected to narrow progressively and close by 2026, indicating that the economy is on track to operate at full potential over the medium term. The government's strategic focus on fiscal prudence, combined with policies to boost industrial diversification and digital transformation, will play a crucial role in ensuring sustained economic expansion in the coming years.

Public Debt: Managing Fiscal Prudence Amid Expansionary Policies

Indonesia's commitment to fiscal responsibility has been a cornerstone of its economic strategy, ensuring macroeconomic stability while accommodating necessary spending for growth. The country's debt-to-GDP ratio has steadily declined, standing at 39.6% in 2023, a continuation of the downward trend from 40.1% in 2022.

This remains well below the statutory debt ceiling of 60%, reinforcing Indonesia's reputation for sound fiscal management. The government's ability to maintain a relatively low debt burden, even as it pursues expansionary fiscal policies, highlights its cautious approach to borrowing and expenditure allocation.

Despite fiscal consolidation efforts, the government recognizes the need to increase targeted spending to support infrastructure development, human capital, and social assistance programs. In 2024, the fiscal deficit is projected to widen to 2.3% of GDP, reflecting a shift towards a moderately expansionary stance. This increase in spending is largely directed towards capital investments in connectivity, energy, and public services, which are expected to yield long-term economic benefits. Additionally, rising government consumption—especially in social programs aimed at reducing poverty and improving education—will contribute to the fiscal impulse of 0.8 percentage points of GDP.

While the deficit is set to expand further to 2.6% of GDP in 2025, it remains well within the fiscal rule's 3% limit, ensuring continued investor confidence in Indonesia's fiscal sustainability. The government has signaled that it intends to gradually consolidate the fiscal deficit beyond 2025 to stabilize public debt levels, ensuring sufficient fiscal space for future economic shocks. Prudent fiscal frameworks, combined with strategic spending allocation, are expected to sustain growth while maintaining debt sustainability.

However, as government expenditures rise, the primary balance, which turned positive at 0.5% of GDP in 2023—the first surplus in nearly a decade—will temporarily return to a deficit of -0.3% of GDP in 2024. This shift reflects the additional fiscal support required to sustain economic momentum amid a challenging global environment. Over the medium term, a careful balance will be needed to manage spending increases without compromising fiscal prudence.

One of the key risks to Indonesia's fiscal outlook is its relatively high debt service-to-revenue ratio, which stands at around 13%. This figure is considerably above the median for emerging markets, underscoring the country's reliance on strong revenue generation to manage its debt obligations effectively. While overall debt levels remain manageable, the burden of debt servicing on government revenues is an area of concern. To address this, authorities have emphasized the importance of revenue mobilization through tax policy enhancements, digitalization of tax administration, and efforts to expand the tax base. Effective implementation of these measures will be crucial to improving fiscal resilience and reducing long-term debt vulnerabilities.

Looking ahead, Indonesia's ability to maintain fiscal credibility while pursuing development objectives will hinge on a well-calibrated fiscal strategy. The government's focus on enhancing revenue collection, optimizing expenditure efficiency, and maintaining a prudent debt profile will be essential in ensuring sustainable public finances. By striking a balance between supporting economic growth and maintaining fiscal discipline, Indonesia is well-positioned to navigate global uncertainties while advancing towards its *Golden Vision 2045* ambitions.

Investment Landscape: The Need for Structural Reforms

Indonesia's investment environment is shaped by a mix of promising opportunities and structural challenges. As Southeast Asia's largest economy, it offers a wealth of natural resources, a rapidly expanding consumer base, and an ambitious infrastructure agenda, making it an attractive destination for foreign investors. The government's commitment to large-scale development projects, particularly the construction of the new capital, Nusantara, has opened new avenues for investment in real estate, construction, energy, and transportation. Additionally, Indonesia's ongoing push for digital transformation and green energy initiatives has further broadened investment opportunities, particularly in renewable energy, electric vehicle production, and industrial down streaming.

Foreign direct investment (FDI) remains a crucial pillar in Indonesia's economic growth strategy. In 2023, FDI inflows reached approximately $21.8 billion, equivalent to about 1.5% of GDP. These investments have been concentrated in sectors such as mining, manufacturing, and financial services, reflecting Indonesia's efforts to enhance industrialization and reduce reliance on raw commodity exports. FDI inflows are expected to grow steadily over the coming years, supported by regulatory reforms aimed at improving the ease of doing business and streamlining investment procedures. However, while the investment outlook remains positive, sustaining and accelerating these inflows will require addressing key structural bottlenecks that have historically hindered investor confidence.

One of the primary concerns for investors is Indonesia's low tax-to-GDP ratio, which stood at just 13% in 2023—significantly below regional benchmarks. The government has set an ambitious goal to increase this ratio by 10 percentage points by 2045, a target that will require substantial tax system improvements. Efforts to achieve this include the proposed establishment of a National Revenue Agency (NRA), digitalization of tax collection processes, and stricter enforcement of tax compliance. However, while these measures are essential for strengthening public finances, they must be carefully executed to avoid creating an excessive tax burden that could deter investment. Ensuring that tax policies remain transparent, predictable, and business-friendly will be critical in maintaining investor confidence.

Beyond fiscal policy, broader structural reforms are needed to enhance Indonesia's investment competitiveness. Labor market inefficiencies, governance issues, and regulatory complexity continue to pose challenges. While Indonesia has made progress in reducing bureaucratic hurdles, further improvements are necessary, particularly in simplifying licensing procedures and ensuring more efficient dispute resolution mechanisms. The country also needs to address concerns related to corruption, which, despite ongoing anti-corruption efforts, remains a deterrent for some investors. Strengthening governance frameworks and reinforcing transparency in public procurement and regulatory decision-making will be key to creating a more investor-friendly business environment.

Indonesia's industrial policies must also evolve to ensure that investment incentives support long-term economic growth without introducing distortions. While the government has adopted measures to encourage domestic value addition—such as requiring certain raw materials to be processed locally before export—it is crucial to balance these policies with the need for open trade and investment flows. Reducing non-tariff barriers, enhancing regulatory certainty, and ensuring that industrial policies do not create market inefficiencies will be essential for sustaining investor interest.

Risks to Growth and Fiscal Stability

Indonesia's economic outlook remains positive, but several downside risks could disrupt growth and fiscal stability. The country is vulnerable to a combination of external and domestic challenges that require careful policy navigation to maintain economic resilience and investor confidence.

External Risks: Trade Balance, Commodity Prices, and Global Financial Conditions

One of the most significant external risks is commodity price volatility. As a major exporter of coal, palm oil, and base metals, Indonesia's trade balance is highly sensitive to fluctuations in global commodity markets. While high commodity prices previously supported a robust trade surplus of $46.5 billion in 2023, softening global demand is expected to slow export growth in 2024. At the same time, import growth is picking up as domestic consumption and investment increase, leading to a projected widening of the current account deficit to -0.9% of GDP. If global energy prices fall sharply or demand from key trading partners weakens further—particularly from China and the US—Indonesia's external sector could face additional pressure.

Another major external challenge is the tightening of global financial conditions. The prolonged period of high interest rates in advanced economies, particularly in the

US, has already led to capital outflows from emerging markets, including Indonesia. This trend puts downward pressure on the rupiah, making it more expensive for Indonesia to service its external debt and raising the risk of financial market volatility. While Bank Indonesia has actively managed exchange rate stability through monetary interventions, further depreciation could increase imported inflation and complicate monetary policy adjustments.

Domestic Risks: Fiscal Sustainability and Policy Execution

Domestically, Indonesia's fiscal framework remains a source of strength, but risks are emerging that could undermine long-term stability. The government's commitment to fiscal prudence has kept debt levels manageable, but maintaining this trajectory requires sustained revenue growth. The country's tax-to-GDP ratio remains one of the lowest in the region at 13%, raising concerns about the government's ability to generate sufficient revenue to fund its ambitious infrastructure and social programs. While tax reform initiatives—including digitalization and the establishment of a National Revenue Agency—aim to improve tax compliance and efficiency, delays in implementation or failure to meet revenue targets could strain public finances.

The IMF has warned that any weakening of fiscal discipline—such as an overreliance on deficit financing or a prolonged period of expansionary spending without revenue enhancements—could erode policy credibility and increase debt servicing costs. The fiscal deficit is projected to reach 2.3% of GDP in 2024 and 2.6% in 2025, still within the fiscal rule's 3% limit, but continued deficit spending without sufficient revenue mobilization could pose long-term risks. Additionally, the growing share of debt service payments relative to government revenue, currently around 13%, is significantly higher than in many emerging markets, underscoring the need for fiscal reforms to prevent crowding out of essential spending.

Geopolitical Risks and External Shocks

Beyond financial risks, geopolitical uncertainties pose a growing threat to Indonesia's economic stability. Rising tensions in global trade, supply chain disruptions, and potential conflicts in key regions could affect commodity exports, disrupt manufacturing inputs, and increase inflationary pressures. A deterioration in global security conditions could also lead to higher oil prices, impacting Indonesia's trade balance and domestic energy costs.

Additionally, unexpected external shocks—such as another pandemic, climate-related disasters, or financial crises in major economies—could disrupt investment flows, weaken consumer confidence, and slow economic momentum. Indonesia's geographical location in the Pacific Ring of Fire further exposes it to natural disasters, which could have fiscal and humanitarian implications if disaster preparedness and mitigation efforts are not strengthened.

Monetary Policy Challenges and Exchange Rate Volatility

Bank Indonesia (BI) has successfully maintained inflation within its target range of 3% ±1%, but the evolving global environment presents challenges for future monetary policy decisions. While inflation remains relatively low, external shocks—such as a sustained increase in US interest rates, a sudden depreciation of the rupiah, or disruptions in global supply chains—could introduce new inflationary pressures. This would force BI to carefully balance interest rate policies to maintain price stability while supporting economic growth.

In response to capital outflows and exchange rate fluctuations, BI has deployed foreign exchange interventions and introduced short-term securities to attract foreign investors. However, if external pressures persist, there could be increased volatility in financial markets, necessitating additional policy adjustments. The central bank's ability to maintain a flexible and data-driven approach will be key to mitigating these risks without causing unnecessary disruptions to domestic credit markets.

Navigating Risks While Maintaining Stability

Indonesia's economic fundamentals remain strong, but the combination of external and domestic risks necessitates proactive policy measures. Strengthening fiscal resilience through improved revenue collection, maintaining a disciplined approach to public spending, and enhancing financial market stability will be critical to mitigating risks. Additionally, continued structural reforms—particularly in governance, taxation, and investment regulations—will help sustain long-term economic growth while ensuring macroeconomic stability in an increasingly uncertain global environment.

Chapter Conclusion: The Road Ahead: Achieving High-Income Status

Indonesia's ambitious goal of reaching high-income status by 2045 requires a transformative approach. The government's "Golden Vision" outlines key reforms necessary to shift from a commodity-dependent economy to one based on high-value-added manufacturing and a skilled workforce. To achieve this vision, Indonesia will need to significantly boost infrastructure investment, improve the quality of education, and reduce barriers to trade and investment.

Achieving high-income status will also require addressing the country's social and environmental challenges. It is of high importance to strengthen social protection programs and ensuring that growth is inclusive. Furthermore, Indonesia's climate goals, including a target of net-zero emissions by 2060, will require substantial investment in renewable energy and carbon-reduction initiatives.

Achieving these goals will not be easy. Structural reforms will be necessary to enhance governance, improve public services, and tackle the barriers that currently limit productivity growth. This will also require strengthening the financial sector, enhancing fiscal management, and boosting international trade relations.

In conclusion, while Indonesia is on a promising growth path, it must remain vigilant to external and domestic risks. With careful management of its fiscal policies, investment in structural reforms, and resilience in the face of global uncertainties, Indonesia has the potential to achieve its vision of becoming a high-income country by 2045. But, as with all ambitious plans, the road ahead will require significant effort and careful policy execution to overcome the risks that lie ahead.

References

- BRICS Think Tank Council: 16th BRICS Summit Kazan Declaration 2024 - https://bricsthinktankscouncil.org/wp-content/uploads/2024/10/16th-BRICS-Summit-Kazan-Declaration-2024.pdf
- ING Think Economic and financial analysis - De-dollarisation: More BRICS in the wall - 23 October 2024
- The BRICS Still Don't Matter by Jim O'Neill - Project Syndicate - https://www.project-syndicate.org/commentary/moscow-brics-summit-expanded-bloc-still-rudderless-and-ineffective-by-jim-o-neill-2024-10
- Vladimir Putin describes BRICS as key element of emerging multipolar world order | TV BRICS, 11.07.24 - ttps://tvbrics.com/en/news/vladimir-putin-describes-brics-as-key-element-of-emerging-multipolar-world-order/
- Financial cooperation and BRICS expansion are on the table as Putin hosts Global South leaders | AP News - https://apnews.com/article/russia-putin-brics-summit-china-india-d672be9b1ec2ffd0fba608e8a6aca790
- Remarks by President Cyril Ramaphosa on the occasion of the BRICS Business Forum Meeting, Kazan, 20 October 2024 - DIRCO - https://dirco.gov.za/remarks-by-president-cyril-ramaphosa-on-the-occasion-of-the-brics-business-forum-meeting-kazan-20-october-2024/
- President Lula's speech during the open plenary session of the BRICS Summit — Planalto - https://www.gov.br/planalto/en/follow-the-government/speeches-statements/2024/10/president-lulas-speech-during-the-open-plenary-session-of-the-brics-summit
- IMF Country Report No. 24/209 on Brazil
- https://www.cia.gov/the-world-factbook/countries/brazil/
- https://www.cia.gov/the-world-factbook/countries/Russia/

- https://www.state.gov/briefings-foreign-press-centers - U.S. Sanctions on Russia FPC Briefing
- https://www.thetimes.com/business-money/energy/article/oil-price-rises-sharply-after-broader-us-sanctions-on-russia-h73388rrl?utm_source=chatgpt.com
- https://www.reuters.com/business/energy/russia-faces-higher-costs-sea-borne-oil-exports-due-new-us-sanctions-2025-01-13/?utm_source=chatgpt.com
- PM's Remarks at the Closed Plenary of the 16th BRICS Summit | Prime Minister of India - https://www.pmindia.gov.in/en/news_updates/pms-remarks-at-the-closed-plenary-of-the-16th-brics-summit/#:~:text=I%20believe%20that%20as%20a%20diverse%20and%20inclusive,one%20that%20works%20in%20the%20interest%20of%20humanity.
- IMF Country Report No. 23/426 on India
- https://www.cia.gov/the-world-factbook/countries/India/
- IMF Country Report No. 24/258 on China
- https://www.cia.gov/the-world-factbook/countries/China/
- Office of the United States Trade Representative - Billing Code 3390-F4 - Notice of Modification: China's Acts, Policies and Practices Related to Technology Transfer, Intellectual Property and Innovation.
- https://www.cia.gov/the-world-factbook/countries/South Africa/
- Egypt & Africa - Egypt values BRICS' invitation to join the bloc: Sisi - https://africa.sis.gov.eg/english/africa-today/african-news/egypt-values-brics-invitation-to-join-the-bloc-sisi/
- IMF Country Report No. 24/98 on Egypt
- https://www.cia.gov/the-world-factbook/countries/Egypt/
- Iran to Join the BRICS Alliance | The Iran Primer - https://iranprimer.usip.org/blog/2023/aug/24/iran-join-brics-alliance
- https://www.cia.gov/the-world-factbook/countries/Iran/
- Ethiopia officially joins BRICS group of emerging economies - EFE - https://efe.com/en/latest-news/2024-01-01/ethiopia-officially-joins-brics-group-of-emerging-economies/
- IMF Country Report No. 24/318 on Ethiopia

- https://www.cia.gov/the-world-factbook/countries/Ehiopia/
- United Arab Emirates joins BRICS Group - https://www.mofa.gov.ae/en/mediahub/news/2023/8/25/25-8-2023-uae-brics
- IMF Country Report No. 24/325 on UAE
- https://www.cia.gov/the-world-factbook/countries/UAE/
- Indonesia officially becomes full member of BRICS bloc – DW – 01/07/2025 - https://www.dw.com/en/indonesia-officially-becomes-full-member-of-brics-bloc/a-71233628#:~:text=The%20BRICS%20bloc%20of%20developing%20nations%20has%20a,on%20Monday%2C%20alongside%20India%2C%20Russia%2C%20China%20and%20others.
- IMF Country Report No. 24/325 on Indonesia
- https://www.cia.gov/the-world-factbook/countries/Indonesia/

www.ingramcontent.com/pod-product-compliance
Lightning Source LLC
Chambersburg PA
CBHW031843200326
41597CB00012B/245
* 9 7 8 1 0 6 8 3 7 9 1 0 9 *